Copyright © 2017 by Jennifer L. Breake

All rights reserved. No part of this book may be reproduced by any mechanical, photographic, or electronic process, or in the form of a phonographic recording; nor may it be stored in a retrieval system, transmitted, or otherwise be copied for public or private use – other than for 'fair use' as brief quotations embodied in articles and reviews – without prior written permission of the publisher.

The author of this book does not dispense medical advice or prescribe the use of any technique as a form of treatment for physical, emotional, or medical problems without the advice of a physician, either directly or indirectly. The intent of the author is only to offer information of a general nature to help you in your quest for emotional and spiritual well-being. In the event you use any of the information in this book for yourself, the author and the publisher assume no responsibility for your actions.

Author's note: To protect the privacy of others, certain names and details have been changed. Some of the stories that appear in this book are composites; individual names and identifying characteristics may have been changed for privacy reasons. Some conversations have been combined to present a more comprehensive treatment of the subject. Nevertheless, these stories reflect authentic discussions I've had with many people over the years.

Out beyond ideas of wrongdoing and rightdoing
there is a field.
I'll meet you there.
When the soul lies down in that grass
the world is too full to talk about.
Let yourself be silently drawn by
the stronger pull of what you really Love.
Your task is not to seek for Love,
but merely to seek and find all the barriers
within yourself that you have built against it.

(Rumi – Sufi Poet)
1207 – 1273

In Memory of my Mothers
Tina Mazalek and Gretha Breakey

Mom, your soul was so soft and gentle and your struggles with this world are over. You were a talented singer and artist, and I just wish we had had more time together. I bet you are singing melodiously with your angelic voice. I love you deeply and I look forward to the day we are both together again.

Gretha, thank you for the unconditional love you gave me for so many years of your life. Your selfless love and caring for my father and his 4 children remains a marvel to me. You are missed by so many and will always be remembered for your kindness, generosity and immense capacity to love. I miss your belly-filled laugh and the special moments we shared together.

I love you both always.

12 STEPS TO LOVING YOU

In Dedication to my Daughter
Julia Frances Breakey

Julia, the day I found out I was pregnant with you, was a day I will never forget. I made a promise to you from that day onwards that I would love and care for you always. Nothing has changed. This remains my promise to you. You are such an inspiration in my life and I see the world differently with you in it. You are one of the kindest, most authentic, sincere and beautiful souls that I have been blessed to share my life with.

I have one remaining everlasting gift to give you, and that is the gift of self-love. I want you to know that you can be anyone you want to be. Don't ever let the inner or external critics drown out your voice. You are unique. There is truly none like you. There is no right or wrong path to take in this life. All you have to do is love yourself deeply and remain true to who you are.

Mother& Daughter

The Inception of 12 Steps to Loving You

It was a calm and balmy day and I was lazily pushing my toes through the warm sand on Camps Bay beach. I remember sitting on the beach and posing a few seemingly serious questions to God. It went something like this.

"God, who am I going to marry when I am older? What is my life's purpose? What would you have me do for you while I am here on earth?" What teenager doesn't think about who she is going to marry one day?

As I sat there on the beach, taking in the sights and sounds of people playing in the waves, seagulls flying overhead and the humdrum of the traffic in the distance, a still small voice inside of me said that I should look at the mountain and say what I saw. My answer was simple. *'I see Table Mountain and the 12 Apostles'*.

'That's right', said the voice. *'What I want you to do is to go and tell the world about my Love and Truth in 12 easy steps'*. 'Sure', I replied. *'I can do that'*. That was over 30 years ago and now I am doing that.

CONTENTS

Introduction Page 7

PHASE 1: ALL ABOUT YOU

Chapter 1: Energy - all that is Page 19
Chapter 2: Who are you? Page 36
Chapter 3: Authenticity Page 45
Chapter 4: Change your thinking Page 56

PHASE 2: ALL ABOUT CHANGE

Chapter 5: Healing the hurt Page 65
Chapter 6: Grounding tools for your journey Page 79
Chapter 7: Soulful integrations Page 89
Chapter 8: Soulful creations Page 103

CHAPTER 3: ALL ABOUT CREATION

Chapter 9: Nature's patterns Page 118
Chapter 10: Wonder-filled meanderings Page 130
Chapter 11: Conscious living Page 141
Chapter 12: Your Sacred Journey Page 152

Afterword *Page 161*
Acknowledgements *Page 165*
About the Author *Page 167*

INTRODUCTION

Where do I begin
To tell the story of how great a Love can be
The sweet Love story that is older than the sea
Where do I start?
(Andy Williams – Love Story)

You are about to embark on one of the greatest adventures that you can ever undertake in this lifetime – the Journey Within. And what you will find will amaze you. The sheer brilliance of who we are is beyond our comprehension.

Step by step you will go deeper and deeper until you reach the very core of your being. No matter what you have been through in this life, you are more than capable of overcoming the difficulties, the wrongful beliefs, the fear and past grievances. All it takes is a willingness to show up each day, no matter how you feel.

This is your time for reconciliation with yourself; a time to forgive yourself for whatever it is you have done that has made you feel unworthy of all the good that this life has to offer.

It is your birth right to experience love, joy, happiness, peace, abundance, wealth, health, success and all the greatness that this life has to offer. *The journey of a thousand miles begins with a single step – Lao Tzu.*

All you have to do is begin, one step at a time. By the time you have worked through all the chapters of the book, you will see an unfolding of who you are. The blossom will open and bloom all in perfect timing. You just need to show up and do the work.

Life is not about struggling and sadness. It is not about the next acquisition or accomplishment. Life is about having fun and experiencing your wholeness. You get to choose how you approach this. You can both feel sorry for yourself and look for sympathy, or you can open your heart and realise that you are 100% accountable for where you are at in your life in this moment. When you take accountability of where you are at, you give yourself the power to make the necessary changes to change your current circumstances. Don't berate yourself for where you are at – you did the best you could with the resources you had. Go easy on yourself; let's go on this journey together.

This book is written in 3 Phases:

1. Phase 1 – All About YOU
2. Phase 2 – All About CHANGE
3. Phase 3 – All About CREATION

YOU – CHANGE – CREATION.

Each chapter goes on its own exploration and at the end of each chapter you will have some questions to answer. This is to help you go within, one step at a time. It will allow you to Stop, Listen, Think, Apply.

Through application your life will start to turn around and head in the direction you choose.

My own path was not straight and easy. It was a web of paths inter-connected with one another. Sometimes my path would take me down a road, only to bring me right back to the same point that I had set out from. I desperately needed to find a way to stop these unwelcome cycles.

What was I thinking and how long had I been feeling this way? The fear and the dread of my reality was all encompassing and constricting. Or was it my reality? Had I created this place where I found myself, or had life just happened to me? I had no idea of really knowing. Not even after being an avid student of metaphysics, spirituality, quantum physics and the mechanics of existence. After fervently following science, religion and spirituality, I was no closer to the truth than I was 30 years ago.

Yet somehow I knew that something within me had changed with all this theoretical knowledge. What was I to believe?

Was it knowledge that had changed me, or the experience I gained through the knowledge and an increased awareness in my consciousness?

Was I to believe that life is just some random existence, and we are all hurtling through space on this round ball called planet earth? To some degree I was too tired to think about it, and quite frankly, I couldn't have cared less. I was just too exhausted.

How could I have foreseen where I was heading with the choices I had made? I had tried to do things on my own steam for far too long and I found myself emotionally, physically and mentally drained. Thankfully the lyrics of a song kept me going – *I get knocked down, but I get up again, you ain't ever going to keep me down.* It is amazing how some songs just stay with you for a lifetime, like Gloria Gaynor's song – *I Will Survive,* which can be heard pelted out by many a rejected ex.

My life was not the existence I had pre-planned, but was I really in control of the outcomes that presented themselves, or was this some cosmic joke by some relentless deity that was in control of all our lives, laughing from the side lines at the futile attempts we make to try and get closer to just a mere glimpse of the truth? When, all along, this deity knows we are on a rollercoaster of non-ever-knowing?

No! I will not allow myself to believe this. After all, I am not a defeatist and I have an insatiable appetite to know the Truth, in whatever form this might present itself.

So I dove headlong into A Course in Miracles and I prayed (like seriously got on my knees and prayed) to my God, the Creator of all Existence, the Source of All.

And it went like this – *dear God, please hear and answer the cries of my heart. Please reveal your true Self to me. The Self of You that I have come to know and love all these years.* Wait! What? Had I just said *'that I have come to know and love all these years'*?

Oh heavenly holy God Almighty! Have I really come to know You - already? I stopped in my tracks to look back at what had been. How had I come this far only to find myself with naught? But was I with naught, I mean, truly with naught?

Sure, I had made a conscious decision to leave my past and most of my belongings behind.

It reminded me of a time when I would end relationships with boyfriends just so they could not hurt me by ending the relationship first. Had I robbed the Universe of its opportunity to take everything from me so that I could learn the duality of having and not having? Perhaps I had orchestrated this. So now what?

Some very distant small voice within me whispered to my soul - *stop, listen, learn and apply*. So I did just that. I stopped, I listened, I learnt and I continue to apply. But what did I hear when I listened? What had I learnt so that I could apply the lessons in this present moment that I am sitting at my desk, putting this all down in writing, with the hope that my words will reach those who need to read this, so that they can also move forward? How can I teach others to make healthy conscious decisions in the now – which truly is all we have? This moment, right now – right here on planet earth.

You might be living some alternative existence elsewhere, but please, don't give it that much attention.

This is the one existence where your consciousness dial is turned up full volume. Your other parallel lives and past life experiences have a place, but not in this present moment. This moment is all we have.

So what exactly do I experience in this existence – about myself, about God? I have come to unconditionally know the following:

1. I am Eternal
2. I am pure Love and Joy
3. I am an Infinite Being
4. I am a Spiritual Being
5. I am a Human Being
6. I am an Emotional Being
7. I am a Physical Being
8. I am a Mental Being
9. I am a Being
10. I simply just I Am
11. I am a Creator
12. The Source of All that Is, loves me unconditionally and does not want me to suffer harm of any kind, but wants me to live a healthy and prosperous life here on earth.

I get it now – I am all things and nothing at the same time. I came into existence on this planet, yet I have always been.

I have never *not been*. So, where have I been? Floating around in some cosmic ship hurtling through time and space?

And then it hit me. Hard. Time and Space do not exist. It is a mind construct to best deal with the way we see our world.

I might not have all the necessary scientific answers, but I have a knowing deep within the core of my Being. I know who I Am. I know I am the manifestation of the eternal Creator, having a human experience. That is the only plausible explanation I can find in a dual world, where non-duality is our ultimate home.

Embrace your Truth of pure Love and Joy, and live from this space in each and every moment. If only it were that simple, but that is our calling. To come back to whom we truly are. We mesh together. God is the Ocean. We are but a drop in the Ocean. We are One and the same.

This does not mean that we do not have challenges in this life. By predisposition, our humanness ensures this.

We need to breathe, eat, live somewhere, and be safe and healthy to ensure longevity here on earth.

We are complicated beings. *As iron sharpens iron, so one person sharpens another (Proverbs)*. Relationships are tricky and oftentimes messy.

We live in a world where everything is energy, and to get something, we need to give something as an energy exchange.

For example, if you want food, you will either give of your time and energy to go and catch it, prepare it and eat it, or you will exchange money (another form of energy) for food.

This is the ebb and flow of life – giving and receiving. If you want Love, then you need to give that which you want to receive.

What has this realisation revealed to me? It shows me that whilst I am the Spark of the Divine, there are still things that are a part of my human existence, such as my ego (which aims at covering my Divinity), my ability to think, formulate opinions, my free will and the ability to live a conscious life here on earth.

Who is laughing now? Some cosmic God who is laughing at our futile attempts at trying to find the Truth, or those of us who have come to realise that we are laughing at ourselves, for what we once searched for, is within us, as us.

The sole and soul intent of this book is to provide you with as much insight and information to bring you to a place of emotional freedom. A place where you are free to choose whatever path it is you wish to walk. The journey is not the destination. The journey is the gentle unfolding of your life's path before you.

This book is about Love and Healing. There is no prelude to any religion or spiritual practice, there is only Love. The universal force-field of Love, because, after all, Love is all there is. Love is your Divine birth right, it is who you are.

All I am here to create is to hold a space for you to experience the Healing that you need to be able to fully Love yourself, just as you are.

It is in:

- looking back at all that has been
- learning to let go and live in the present moment
- understanding that you are an energetic being
- finding peace where you previously had none, and
- in the new creation, your co-creation, of what is to come

that you will find the *life changing message* which lies at the heart and soul of this book.

12 Steps to Loving You is about stripping away all the layers that you are not, one step at a time. It is about lifting the veil that is between your unconscious and conscious mind.

Have you seen the movie Shrek where Donkey says that Shrek is like an onion, in that he has multiple layers? Well, I guess Donkey got it right because we are all like onions in that we all have multiple layers. By stripping away the layers, you will once again come face to face with your true identity and core essence.

I am honored and privileged to be sharing this journey with you. It is fun and easy, and also challenging, but so long as you approach it one step at a time, the rewards will be endless.

It is a wondrous Joyful journey. So sit back, get a cup of coffee, your journal, and get ready to prepare for a soulful journey of Love, Healing, acceptance, appreciation and gratitude.

You are about to embark on a journey of self-discovery, learning to let go of grievances and learning to love yourself with a depth that you never knew was possible.

As with any journey, you need to be well-prepared, so here are a few tips for you before embarking on this adventure:

1. approach this inner work with an open mind and a loving heart
2. see probabilities and possibilities as opportunities for growth
3. create a time and space for you to do this work
4. be prepared for your life to shift from a state of lack of love (which is fear) to one of Love and Joy
5. be patient, kind and gentle with yourself throughout the process

You can do this. It is your birth right to live a happy, Joyful, loving and abundantly successful life.

Don't be robbed of this opportunity to totally love who you are, just as you are, right here and right now.

Just by reading this book, it means that you want more out of life and that you want to learn to live in the peace and Joy of loving yourself completely.

It is not possible to love your neighbour unless you love yourself first.

For everyone to play their part in this world we need to love ourselves first.

Only then does it become an automatic way of being towards loving others. Everyone is afraid of something, and oftentimes this is the fear of loving so deeply because we fear getting hurt. Don't let this stop you from exploring the depths of your love for yourself and others. You are Love personified. Embrace it, live it and share it with the world.

Eternally yours,

Jennifer L. Breakey

PHASE I

ALL ABOUT YOU

CHAPTER 1
ENERGY – ALL THAT IS

Everything is energy and that's all there is to it.
Match the frequency of the reality you want and you cannot
help but get that reality. It can be no other way.
This is not philosophy.
This is physics.
(Albert Einstein)

The above quote is disputed as to whether or not it was said by Albert Einstein. It makes no difference to me whether or not Albert Einstein did or did not say this. The meaning still holds true for me. Everything is energy. This is science. Undisputed.

So how does this knowing effect the way we see ourselves, our lives and the universe as a whole? And what is energy?

My tenacity to learn absolutely everything possible there is to know about how *everything is energy* has taken me on a remarkable journey of discovery.

In June 2008, I certified as a Reiki Master and received the necessary attunements and knowledge of Shoden (level 1) Okuden (level 2) and Shinpiden (Master Level). This was in the Usui system of natural healing.

Although I am a certified Reiki Master, I am not a practicing Reiki Master Practitioner, other than using the techniques on myself.

I undertook these studies to learn more about energy healing and the way we can channel energy to bring about changes in our lives. This formed part of my learning of energy being all there is.

It is far better to experience something than to sit and only focus on theoretical knowledge. Notwithstanding, theory has its place and value, but only if converted to application. Imagine you had to learn all there is to know about chocolate ice-cream. Wouldn't you rather eat the chocolate ice-cream than only learn about it?

Think about the light switch. You put it on and the room is lit up. You do not think about how or why this happens, you are just grateful for the electric current that allows this to be. Sometimes, however, it is beneficial to delve a bit deeper and found out why some things are the way they are.

The following fields have been my fields of study in Energy – All That Is:

1. A Course in Miracles
2. Shamanism
3. Reiki
4. Chakra Cleansing and Balancing

These are the foundations upon which I have built the integration of mind, body and spirit.

I have also studied quantum physics, metaphysics and other new thought conscious ways of thinking.

There is no right or wrong way to learn about energy.

If you wish to expand your knowledge of energy healing, energy medicine and energy – all that is, then delving into energy areas of interest will enhance your knowledge base and give you the opportunity for wonderful experiences.

They are each dynamic on their own and together they form part of a greater whole.

A Course in Miracles

A Course in Miracles is a complete self-study spiritual thought system and is the foundation for Inner Peace. It is a three-volume curriculum consisting of a Text, Workbook for Students, and Manual for Teachers.

It teaches that the way to universal love and peace, or remembering God, is by undoing guilt through forgiving others.

The Course focuses on the healing of relationships and making them holy. It emphasizes that it is but one version of the universal curriculum, of which there are 'many thousands'.

Even though the language of the Course is that of traditional Christianity, it expresses a non-sectarian, non-denominational spirituality.

A Course in Miracles therefore is a universal spiritual teaching and not a religion.

Shamanism

Shamanism is an ancient healing tradition and way of life and Shamanic teachings focus on our connection to nature and all of creation.

Because modern culture doesn't have a role for the shamanic archetype, many people who grow up outside indigenous villages are shamans and don't even know it.

Many naturally wind up in healing professions, such as medicine, psychology, or life coaching. Unfortunately, the systems of Western medicine and psychology leave little room for a shaman to practice his or her natural healing art.

While not everyone can apprentice with a traditional shaman or become an official shaman today, it is still possible to practice the techniques of shamanism for gaining physical, mental, and spiritual health, accumulating vitality and power, and for self-development.

I attended an Ayahuasca ceremony and was amazed at the results, which brought me into a closer awareness of who I am and how best to walk my journey of self-love. Cautionary note – this ceremony is not for everybody, so make sure that if you attend an Ayahuasca ceremony that you are with a reputable Shaman.

Ayahuasca is an Amazonian plant mixture that is capable of inducing altered states of consciousness, usually lasting between 4 to 8 hours after ingestion.

Reiki

Reiki is a Japanese word meaning universal life energy. Rei means a universal, transcendental spirit, a boundless essence. Ki translates to life force energy. This life force energy can be defined as that energy which resides and acts in all created matter, animal, vegetable or mineral. In all cultures and religions there is a name or concept which corresponds to the meaning of Ki in Reiki, although some of the theories may be quite different. The most well-known of these are:

Chi   found in Chinese medicine e.g. acupuncture and Qigong
Prana   found in the Hindu Upanishads and yoga
Light   found in Christian teachings

Everything that has life contains Ki and radiates it. The person who has received the Reiki attunements or initiation has their body's energy channels opened in a way that connects them to the Universe's limitless source of Ki. Reiki is healing energy in its truest sense.

Chakra Cleansing and Balancing

Learning about the chakra system is a part of the Reiki teachings. Both the chakra system and Reiki are focal points to allow you to focus on energy healing in a disciplined manner.

Chakra is a Sanskrit word meaning 'wheel'.

There are seven major chakras in the body which starts at the base of the spine and goes up to the crown of the head.

The chakra system is complex and requires focused study in order to appreciate its subtleties fully.

Your chakras can become stagnant or blocked when their dials are turned up too high or turned down too low, so it is important that you know how to intuit the state of your chakras so that perfect balance and harmony can be achieved.

The language of the Universe

The beauty of life is that you get to choose the path that leads you home, all the while knowing that there is a place of pure energy that exists, and we all need to learn to speak the language of this pure energy. So, what is the Universal Language? It is the language of our *emotions and feelings*.

Our emotional makeup is central throughout all beings. Your emotions are the language of the Universe and the Universe responds to your emotional state. The Universe responds to who you are, not to what you want, and who you are is largely influenced by your emotional state.

If everything is indeed energy, then how do you tap into your various energy states, and change them from low frequencies to those of higher ones?

The book The Secret says you should drop a bit of Joy into any low frequency you experience, and this will elevate your state of being.

This does not always work.

For example, when you are upset or angry at someone or something, are you able to drop some Joy into the situation? It is not as easy as it seems.

The best way to deal with this is to first identify the part of you that feels angry. Do this by sitting quietly and seeing yourself as the big blue sky and your emotions as the clouds that float on by. See the anger come into view and then float on by so that you no longer see or feel them. Place no emotional attachment to what you see. The Universe truly does respond to your emotions and feelings. Think of it like this. Your emotions and feelings are the magnet that draws your experiences to you.

So when you feel in a state of lack and want abundance, you will not achieve this shift until you face your fear of lack and let it float into view and then let it float out again. This takes practice and discipline, but if you want something dearly enough, you will put in the time and energy to work on your emotional wellbeing.

There are two major energy fields. The first is Love and the second is Fear. You get to choose which one you reside in at any given moment in time. You cannot be in both. There is no overlap.

Think of it like this. When you wake up every day, you get to choose which slippers to put on; your Love Slippers or your Fear Slippers? Because most people are not awake or only awakening to what is beyond the physical world, they tend to make this choice unconsciously.

People tend to like their old trusted pair of slippers, and if you are more comfortable with the way you used to feel, that is fear-based, then you will instinctively reach for your Fear Slippers.

How about turning this into a game? Each morning you get up, say *thank you* to the Universe 3 times, and then consciously look at your feet and ask yourself this question: - 'what slippers am I going to wear today'? Then consciously reach for the Love Slippers, and although they are fairly new and hardly worn yet, give them some time. Pretty soon you will be reaching for them sub-consciously, because loving yourself will become second nature.

The way you feel will dictate which Slippers you instinctively reach for. If you are feeling fearful, for whatever reason, you will reach for the Fear Slippers, and you will attract more fearful situations by the paths you choose to walk. If you wear the Love Slippers, you will attract more Love-filled situations.

Everything is energy, from the animate to the inanimate objects in life. Even words hold their own energetic vibration. Let's take a look at the rice or water experiment.

Two containers (one holding water or rice) had the words Love and Hate stuck on them.

These containers were left for a few days and upon examining the containers after a few days, it was found that the rice or water containers with the word Love on them, was aesthetically beautiful.

The containers with the words Hate on it were not pleasing to the eye. What made this difference? Simply explained, the vibration of each word (the meaning, feeling, emotion which we give to both words) created this difference.

Can you imagine the effect that this can have on your own health? If you hold angry unloving thoughts towards yourself vs holding loving thoughts, what impact do you think this will have on your health and general wellbeing? Not a pleasant thought and a strong enough one that should make you sit up and take note of what you are thinking.

Everything is energy, from your feelings, emotions, thoughts, words, actions, character and destiny. It is all energy and you get to choose what your energy blueprint will be in this life.

You need to learn to be intuitively aware of your energetic emotive states as you go about your day. Every few hours or so, simply focus on what you are feeling and make the necessary shifts you need to, if you feel that your energetic states are draining and toxic.

To help you have a visionary focal point for scanning your body, let's look at your 7 major chakras.

You do not have to be spiritual or religious to benefit from using your 7 major chakras as scanning points in your body. These 7 chakras run from the base to of your spine to the crown of your head.

The top 3 major chakras are to do with your *thought and logic processes*. They allow you to formulate pictures in your mind, but you can only invite these pictures into your life if you breathe emotions into them. By imbuing emotions into your thoughts, you give them life.

The bottom 3 major chakras are to do with your *emotions*.

The 4th chakra (Heart Chakra) is the chakra which joins them together.

Together these 7 major chakras give you a formula for wholeness and wellbeing. The location of the chakras in the body gives meaning to their respective levels of consciousness.

Our universe is made up of spinning wheels of energy and in the same way, our chakras are spinning wheels of life. Their spinning comes from the intersection of 2 basic currents, one from the above and one from below. As these currents pass between the chakras, the chakra centres spin like gears.

Your first major chakra is your Base Chakra and the colour associated with it is red. This chakra represents your physical will to be, tuning into the here and now. The Base or Root Chakra governs understanding of the physical dimension, the quantity of physical energy and vitality. It is the centre of the will to live.

    Location   coccyx
    Element   earth
    Instinct   survival

Your second major chakra is your Sacral Chakra and the colour associated with it is orange. This chakra represents your lower creative centre, your reproductive system and your sexual energies. This is the emotional and creative centre that influences the reproductive and the muscular system. It governs sensation, emotion, desire, pleasure and sexuality and controls many personality functions.

    Location   below naval
    Element   water
    Instinct   sexuality

Your third major chakra is your Solar Plexus Chakra and the colour associated with it is yellow. This chakra represents your self-awareness centre and it is your emotional engine room. This is the centre of intellect and personal power and is the key to our inner power, allowing us to fulfil our dreams, have autonomy and be individuals. It is also the centre of empathy.

    Location   solar plexus
    Element   fire
    Instinct   power

Your fourth major chakra is your Heart Chakra and the colour associated with it is green. This chakra represents higher love and brings balance between your mind, body and spirit. This is the centre of compassion and is the bridge between the physical and spiritual energies, acting as a mediator between the chakras.

    Location   chest
    Element   air
    Instinct   love

Your fifth major chakra is your Throat Chakra and the colour associated with it is blue. This chakra represents your higher creative centre of communication linking with the mental body and self-expression. This is our centre of communication and assimilation. It is here that we take responsibility for ourselves and where we squeeze through the bottleneck of to realise, or openly acknowledge our spirituality.

    Location   throat
    Element   sound
    Instinct   physical expression

Your sixth major chakra is your Brow Chakra and the colour associated with it is indigo. This chakra represents the perceptive centre of higher comprehension and overview and promotes intuition.

This chakra is also known as the 3rd eye. This chakra is linked to the level of the sub-conscious mind that controls intuitive perception, creative imagination and visualisation.

    Location   the centre of the forehead
    Element   light
    Instinct   truth

Your seventh major chakra is your Crown Chakra and the colour associated with it is violet. This chakra represents the spiritual will to be, self-realisation, calmness and peace. This chakra allows for the integration of total personality with life and spiritual aspects of mankind. This is the centre of our most spiritual essence. It helps us connect with our Higher Selves.

    Location   the crown on the top of the head
    Element   thought
    Instinct   universal ethics

A great practice is to sit quietly and *go within* your body. Start scanning from the base of your spine and ask yourself these 4 questions at each chakra point:

1. What does my chakra feel like?

2. What does my chakra look like?

3. Are there dark patches in my chakra?

4. Is my chakra spinning smoothly?

5.   How fast or slow is my chakra spinning?

These are questions to help you get in tune with your chakras and it does become easier with practice. If you feel unease in your chakra, then you know that this is an opportunity for you restore balance to your life.

The aim here is to find balance and harmony through the practice of Chakra Cleansing and Balancing. You can do this yourself, or you can go to a Reiki Master who can help you cleanse and balance your chakras.

This is a wonderful tool to find areas where you are blocked in life, so that you can release these blockages and move in the flow of glory of all that is.

Here are some basic questions to ask yourself regarding the energy levels in your own life. Answer them as honestly as you can, and fill the answers in with pencil. This will allow you to come back a few weeks or months later, as your situation changes from time to time.

It is important to note that there are no right or wrong answers, things are just the way they are, but you need a starting point to start attuning yourself to the energy levels in your body. Remember, this is all about giving yourself the gift of love, and one of the greatest gifts you can give yourself, is the ability to be aware of the state of your emotional, physical, mental and spiritual wellbeing.

Have fun with this. No one else is going to be reading your notes. This is just for you, so that you can have a solid foundation to begin your life's journey of true self love.

YOU AND YOUR ENERGETIC STATE OF BEING

1. What is your current state of energy levels in your body?

2. Which areas of your life are draining you of your energy and what can you do to change this? These areas can be:
    a. Your home life
    b. Your work
    c. Your relationships
    d. Your worry about finances
    e. Your health
3. Are you aware of energy parasites in your life? These are those relationships that drain you of your energy.

4. What can you do about the energy parasites in your life, that will not hurt the other party, but that will empower you to be free of toxic relationships?

5. Do you have a practice that you can do, such as meditation that will help you bring back balance and harmony to your life?

6. If you answered 'no' to the question above, what forms of energy healing or other practices can you do to help you maintain equilibrium in your life?

7. Do you harbour anger or resentment to anyone in your life? This can be a major cause for energy lethargy.

8. If you harbour anger, resentment, judgement, criticism, hatred, impatience or any other negative energy towards yourself or anyone else, what can you do to release yourself and the other party/-ies involved?

9. What is the level of peace and harmony in your life?

10. How can you improve the level of peace and harmony in your life?

11. Is your life grounded in some form of religious or spiritual activity? This can be meditation, taking walks nature, painting, yoga or any other form of activity that brings you back to your state of centeredness.

12. What changes, if any, can you make to your current diet and exercise regime?

AFFIRMATION FOR CHAPTER 1

Everything I see and do not see is energy. I have full control over the energy in my body, surroundings and circumstances.

CHAPTER 2
WHO ARE YOU?

Do you know what you are?
You are a manuscript of a divine letter.
You are a mirror reflecting a noble face.
This universe is not outside of you.
Look inside yourself;
everything that you want,
you are already that.
(Rumi)

I remember the first time someone asked me this question – Jennifer, who are you? I was busy on a management training program, and this program was geared to challenge the way you think.

I looked at the training facilitator as though she was bonkers. I mean, could they not see that I am a human being called Jennifer? At this time I was an HR Manager at a large printing company in Cape Town. To appear wise, I answered *I am Light*. After all, this was the answer they were looking for, right?

And I was right – this was the answer they were looking for. Giving this answer, however, made me feel like a fraud.

Surely I should have said I am the HR Manager, as that was my consciousness at the time? Instead, I projected something of meaning without first having the experience.

Looking back at this incident I can see how I desperately needed to fit in. This did not serve my journey of awakening in any way. In fact, I was scared people would get to see that I did not know it all. I have now come to know that we have the answers that we are searching for, within us, we have just drowned out the voice with daily distractions and our ego.

I call this space of knowing within us, our quantum pool of knowledge. We swim in different parts of the pool, so our learnings are different from each other.

Are you your body, or your mind, or your soul, or something beyond this physical realm? Or are you all of those things rolled into one? Some people believe we are what you see and they cannot see past this reality. Others have a knowing that we are more than what we see, but they do not know what to call this.

Sadly, so many people try to validate their existence by accumulating things along the way.

They chase the big cars, big houses, corner office jobs, the flashy bling, the huge bank balance, power, lust and greed and so much more. This is a dangerous breeding ground for corruption.

The world has a fierce way of keeping you asleep.

It bombards you with bad news, false advertising (to be a true man you should drive this car, use this mobile phone etc.), and it tries to convince you that you are inadequate at every corner.

Without a seconds thought, people run off to the stores to buy the latest gadget, designer clothes (now I am not knocking designer clothes – who doesn't like wearing designer jeans, right?), but the point here is not to berate these things, but rather to highlight the unnecessary consumerism trap that so many have fallen into.

That was me not so long ago, although it does seem a lifetime ago. As a single mother from when my daughter was 3 months old, I lived in a numb state of depression and despair. Fear was all-consuming and the responsibility of raising my daughter on my own was the driver for my fear.

I accumulated a lot along the way. I wanted to make sure that my daughter lacked for nothing. We landed up living in a big 4 bed-roomed home with 1 large study, 3 bathrooms, a double garage, kitchen, scullery, swimming pool, sitting area, lounge, entertainment area – which was all possible because I had worked hard and climbed the corporate ladder through my career path. All these things made me feel safe and secure. What a false sense of being. At the time I did not see it like that. If you had told me that I was allowing things to validate my existence, I would most likely have responded in defiance and even hurt.

It was in this home that I had my true dark night of my soul experience. I had just been released from hospital for a stomach ailment, and I had eaten a cheese and onion sandwich. I regretted eating the onion the moment that I had consumed the sandwich. At just after midnight I woke up and was wide awake. I was in slight discomfort, but I could not make sense of what was happening. Why was I this wide awake? There was a sense that something greater than me was about to go down, and I was all in to find out what this was all about.

I sat up and felt the urge to get a pen and notepad and start writing, and I did this for the next 4 hours. I had a sudden sense of urgency to write down everything I believed I had done wrong in this lifetime. The unforgiveness and grievances I held towards myself and others.

I could not believe that after 4 hours of writing, there was still more to write down. Had I been such a bad person, that I could fill so many pages of my perceived wrongdoings? It took me a period of about 3 weeks to finish this list. I would find myself in a conversation at work, and then suddenly another grievance would come to mind, and I would make a mental note to write it in my book when I got home. It was as though I was purging myself of all this guilt, shame, fear, unforgiveness, untruths and a deep sense of separation from life and God, my Creator of All.

It was a short while after this incident that I realised who I truly am.

I am not my things, qualifications, status, financial standing or any other materialistic possession that I had acquired over the years. I am not my guilt, fear, shame, disappointments, hurts, betrayals, or the seeming confusion that would pervade my thoughts.

I am me, the very essence and core of Jennifer Leonie Breakey. After I stripped away the layers of grief, hurt, disappointments, anger, frustration, unforgiveness, betrayal and all the energetic things that weighed me down, I was left with the pure essence of me, Love and Joy.

Now I know this sounds blissfully heavenly, but it came at a price. I knew I no longer could be the person I was before this experience.

I ceremoniously burnt the book I had used for the past 3 weeks, letting go of all that had once hidden myself from me. Or to put it another way, *hidden my Self from me.*

The veil was lifted, the shroud removed. The scales fell off my eyes, and I knew I was more than all these trappings. If I was more than my physical form, how else could I identify my being? I realised that this would be questionable to some friends and family, and so I did not talk about it much. Have you ever experienced a shift in yourself that you know people would not accept? It was this feeling I had. I have since come to realise that it is okay to let go of toxic and non-directional relationships (regardless whether they are family or friends).

I no longer allow myself to spend time with those who just want to question my every choice I make. Invariably they only hear what they want to hear. I am deeply happy to just be. Me.

So many people focus on others because they do not want to focus on their own journey, as it is too painful. Be sensitive to these souls, as they too have a journey to travel.

We are all Divine Sparks of Life and at the very core of our beings we are all pure Love and Joy. A deep sense of knowing is all I can give you as an explanation, and I am aware that this might not be enough for some people, so I would encourage you to have an open mind as you read this book. There are so many possibilities that exist to explain who you are in this wonderful tapestry called Life.

When you feel lost and all alone and the burdens of this world weigh heavy on your soul, just remember that you are Love, Light and a beautiful soul, connected to absolutely everyone and everything in this great Web of Life. Don't let the trappings of this world hold you back from living your truth.

There is absolutely nothing wrong with having wealth, health and prosperity. It is the non-attachment to these things that is important. So go out there, be brave, be you! Because you are worth it and the world needs you in it.

Many people say I will be happy when …. But the truth is that you can live in a state of happiness right now, regardless of what you do or do not have.

Sometimes the person we need to forgive the most is ourselves.
Stop berating yourself for past mistakes. Step up to the plate, take a swing at that ball, and smash all your perceived failures out of the ball park. They do not define who you are.

You are a magnificent and wondrous person, worthy of love and acceptance. You have as much right to be here on earth as does the next person. Don't lose that knowing.

WHO ARE YOU?

1. Who are you?

2. Is it possible that you can be more than just your physical body?

3. Have you ever thought of someone and then you bumped into them, or your phone rang and it was them? Or have you had some other chance happening? If so, what do you think created this?

4. Do you believe you are a beautiful being?

5. If you answered 'no' to the above, what are the characteristics and traits that you do not like within yourself, and how do you think you could turn this negative picture about you into a positive one?

6. Do you believe that you are a harsh critic of yourself?

7. List 5 of your weak points.

8. List 5 of your strong points.

9. Which was easier to answer, your weak or strong points? Most people find it easier to list their weak points. This highlights that you need to bring love to those areas that you are self-critical of.

10. Can you look in the mirror and truthfully tell yourself that you are beautiful, or do you feel that this would be fake?

11. Who would you like to be? What perceived 'better' version of yourself would you like to show to the world? Can you start being that person today?

AFFIRMATION FOR CHAPTER 2

I am not my insecurities or fears. I am loved beyond measure by Source who does not judge me in any way.

CHAPTER 3

AUTHENTICITY

To thine own self be true – William Shakespeare
The privilege of a lifetime is to become who you truly are - Carl Jung

This quote is deeply entrenched in my life and has become one of my life's mottos. When I first read this it made me question if I was in fact being true to myself. I did not like the answer I gave myself.

What is authenticity and why the hype about it? An authentic person is a genuine person, one who is themselves without adding frills and untruths to their persona. They are the 'what you see is what you get' person. They might have positive affirmations which are great grounding works for being who you want to be, but they are realistic in their approach to their own authenticity.

Authentic people are optimistic and this is far more beneficial than just being positive. Positivity does not make something so. A change in perception does.

I am not knocking positive affirmations. They certainly can help you shift your perception from a negative state to a positive one, but positivity is not the ultimate catalyst for true change.

Change comes through repetition of new behaviour. Creating new dendrites in your brain (neurological pathways) takes repetition of behaviour and not just saying positive affirmations over and over again (more on this in Chapter 11), although as previously mentioned, they do help.

To be authentic is to be your genuine self. The problem we face today is that some people just do not know who they are. If you are battling with your own self-identity, then go back and revisit Chapter 2 and look for some resonance within its pages.

Sit quietly and contemplate what your life would be like if you stripped yourself of everything you own, take away all those things that are linked to your social status, and just sit there and imagine yourself marooned on an island. Who would you be without your trappings? What would you see differently? What feelings would rise to the surface? Are you masquerading behind things? Are you comfortable with your own company?

Many people battle with this and they fill the void of time with work, time out with family and friends, television, gaming, gambling, drinking and all other forms of addictions or activities that can distract them from spending time alone.

It was not until my late 40's that I started understanding what it was like to live an authentic life.

When I was younger, fitting in was of paramount importance to me, even if this meant not being true to myself.

I was funny, charming, loving, kind, and generous and although I am still those things today, I am now those things without having to people please or fit in. I am those things because I choose to be without having to fake it until I make it.

What clouded my judgement of myself and how did I break free from this? I think the biggest factor that played out in my life was the fear of not fitting in, not belonging or not being lovable.

My mother had left my life when I was 2 years old and at a subconscious level I must have wondered if it was because I wasn't lovable that she left. My adult brain could compute that this was not the case, but the entry point of the hurt (at 2 years old) I could not compute this. The rejection and abandonment was palpable. I knew that if I want to live an authentic life, I had to let go of the grievances I held against my mother and other people that had hurt me.

I dealt with hurt by being overly happy, kind, a people pleaser and someone you could always count on to help you, even if it was to the detriment of my own self and health. While I was living this inauthentic existence, I was carrying within me, the deep burden of unresolved anger. I also very rarely showed my true feelings to anyone else.

At the end of 2008 I went to see an energy healer and was told that I had deep-seated anger within me, and although he could clear this, he felt that he should not and that I needed to go through this learning process.

I chose to let it go, all of it. The hurt, the rejection and the abandonment and it was not easy. Every few years I seemed to be dealing with the same thing. Had I not previously let this go? Why did I have to revisit these issues over and over again when I had previously worked so hard at letting them go?

Was there a formula to apply when letting these issues go and had I not applied it correctly? I had absolutely no idea.

Then I realised – nature abhors a vacuum. So when I had let it go, I did not replace the hurt, rejection and abandonment with anything. I just looked at it, forgave those who needed forgiving (even if it included forgiving myself) and thought 'there you go, done and dusted'. I am healed. And at some level, I had removed surface issues, but not pulled out the roots that went deep into my psyche.

It was time for emotional freedom and to set myself free from the hurt and pain. I no longer wanted to live like this. I threw the towel in. I quit my job. I got rid of most of my earthly belongings and made a conscious decision that I was never going to allow myself to be manipulated by anyone again.

I took ownership of my life and decided to follow my dreams. I was going to walk my truth, wherever that might take me, without fear or shame.

And this has not been an easy path to take. I realise that I had taken a drastic approach which placed a lot of burden on some people in my life and that was never my intention.

However, had I not made a choice to make some drastic changes in my life, it would not be unfolding in the way that it is.

I have known for over 30 years that my reason for being here is *to bring love and create a space for healing to occur*. My career stopped me following my dreams, passions and it slowly eroded away at my authentic being. I lived in constant fear in my job, not knowing when the next knife would be thrust into my back (had I called this into existence to get me to change direction and quit my job?).

I created the situations that led to this decision, so although it took me about a year to truly forgive the grievances I held against certain individuals in the workplace, I realised that they were just playing out their role in my life, which is now allowing my story to unfold in the way that it is destined to unfold.

I am now able to send them Love and Blessings and wish them no harm. I could not do this a year ago. I wish them well and pray that they will find the happiness and peace they need to live a fully actualised life.

We are all connected, and when one person hurts we all hurt. If I hurt them by holding grievances against them, then I am hurting myself. I now live my life authentically. What you see is what you get.

I am deeply connected with who I am and I would not change this for anything. I embrace all that I am without any defence or trepidation.

Being authentic is something that you consciously need to work at. If you feel yourself falling back into people pleasing, don't be hard on yourself. Just see where you are compromising your own self in the situation, and make the necessary shifts to get you back on the right path.

How do you change from being a people pleaser and fearful of showing your true colours to others? I am not going to tell you that it is an easy part of your inward journey, but I am going to tell you that you are not alone in this journey. There are many others just like you who are facing the same challenges.

One of the barriers that you will come up against is the hardest one you will ever have to face. Part of the challenge of living an authentic life is that you will not be able to achieve this if you do not love yourself as you are, right here and right now.

I know just how hard it can be to forgive yourself for all the things you have done that has hurt others or yourself. Regardless of whether I can show you that all of this hurt is an illusion, it will not make the pain you feel about the situations any less difficult to deal with.

Learning to love you is a road that some people travel and then take a detour and leave the road because they do not like what they see.

The good things are that if you persist with this journey, the terrain will change as you keep moving along this road.

12 STEPS TO LOVING YOU

It is often easier to love others than it is to love yourself. If you can just remember that everyone does the best they can with what they have at any given moment in time, then this must logically apply to you just as much as it applies to them.

So please don't be hard on yourself. You have done the best you can to get to where you are today and the great news is that it is never too late to change the course of your life. Being authentic means showing up as yourself wherever you go.

Here are 5 steps to help you live an authentic life:

1. Redefine your values – it's hard to behave in an authentic way if you do not know what you value and desire.
2. Foster an open mind.
3. Fill in the blank: If you really knew me you'd know this about me:

   _____
   _____
   _____
   _____
   _____
   _____
   _____
   _____

4. Notice when you are being inauthentic.
5. Trust your intuition.

Being authentic means coming from a real place within. It is when our actions and words are congruent with our beliefs and values. It is being ourselves, not an imitation of what we think we should be or have been told we should be.

Part of knowing ourselves is knowing what we believe in. Throughout our childhoods we are picking up messages that become part of our belief system. Left unchallenged, we can walk around thinking that these beliefs are our own. Part of finding our authentic self is sorting through these beliefs to find out which are truly our own.

Do our beliefs come from a mature, healthy, grounded place within us, or are they remnants from our childhood, coming from an insecure place?

Being authentic is more than being real; it is finding what is real. And what is real for me will be quite different than what is real for you.

There is no judgement or value attached to either: it simply is what it is for each of us. If your sexual orientation, spiritual beliefs or chosen path is different than mine, this is okay.

When we are both living from our authentic selves, our differences do not challenge us. There are no judgements. I honour the authentic you and you honour the authentic me. I see the Divine Spark in you and I acknowledge the same Divine Spark in me. We are just walking a different path, heading towards the same destination.

Just imagine how congested the roads would be, if we all travelled the same path?

YOU AND YOUR AUTHENTICITY

1. What does authenticity mean to you?

2. Are you living a truly authentic life? If not, in which areas of your life can you show up more authentically?

3. Are you a people pleaser, and if so, what are the driving forces behind your people pleasing?

4. Are you confident in who you are and comfortable in your own skin? If not, in what areas do your life do you lack self-confidence?

5. Have you ever done the inner work to find out who you truly are, and if so, what was the experience like for you? If you had a negative fearful experience, don't let that stop you from doing the work now.

6. Briefly describe what you remember about your childhood. Were there any traumas that you can remember, and if so, who do you need to release through forgiveness? UNICEF states that the early childhood years from birth through to the age of 8 years, are formative in terms of intelligence, personality and social behaviour. The first two years are particularly crucial. According to UNICEF, people develop best intellectually, emotionally and inter-personally when their formative years are free of repression, natural disasters, malnutrition, polluted water and armed conflict. This question will give you a deep insight into how your life might have been adversely affected due to circumstance, and you will notice unresolved issues which needs releasing. This is very important when it comes to loving yourself completely.

7. Briefly describe your formative years as an adolescent, which is the period between the onset of puberty and the cessation of physical growth; roughly from 11 to 19 years of age. (Formative is a word that describes something that made you who you are.) You might call your adolescence your formative years because that time period had such a strong influence on the rest of your life.

8. What are the values and beliefs that you hold dear? Do you live up to these? If not, why not?

AFFIRMATION FOR CHAPTER 3

My actions and words are congruent with my beliefs and values. I always show up authentically, and unashamedly so.

CHAPTER 4
CHANGE YOUR THINKING
– CHANGE YOUR LIFE

For as he thinketh in his heart, so is he – Proverbs

The late Dr. Wayne Dyer was the first person to introduce me to *change your thinking – change your life.* From the knowledge that everything is energy, including our words, it stands to reason that our thoughts are energy too. I have become quite astute at noticing energetic shifts in my physical body when my thinking is not congruent to my authenticity. It really is uncanny.

When you learn to watch your thoughts like a hawk you will notice the effects that your thinking has on your body. The interesting part for me is that thoughts don't all show up in the same place in my body. For example, fear sits in my gut and Joy in my heart area.

Through my own personal experience, I have come to believe that what you consistently think about becomes your reality. It is always so. Without exception. I decided to put this to the test and the results were astonishing.

Many years ago I had a huge falling out with a friend, and with so much anger and hurt, I intended that she leave Cape Town.

I was clearly not emotionally aware at the time, as I did not know that this was so destructive and could easily have been resolved, but this was the only way that my bottled-up self could deal with the situation. It was no major surprise when I found out that my friend was relocating back to her home town and leaving Cape Town. Somehow this did not help me in any way, as I knew that I was going to miss my friend, regardless of our differences. I believe that because I was so intently focused on this for months, and because the thoughts I was having had the full attention of all my emotions, this situation became my reality.

At another time, I asked the Universe for two things, a boyfriend and a new job, I was really specific in what I wanted in both, and after a short while I got both, exactly per my request. Coincidence? I think not.

With this new found reality, I began playing with this, and so can you. However, as a cautionary side-line I will say this. Be careful of what you ask for, as you just might get it, and it is not always what you think it will be. This has been my experience. I have learnt to be precise in what I ask for, as the impact can be somewhat derailing if you have not thought it through.

Changing your thinking to change your life is so much more than this. Your belief system is so engrained in you, that the thoughts you think about certain things are habitual.

To delve into your belief system takes time and sometimes it helps to do this with an experienced professional who can help you identify your current belief system. It is by no means an easy process.

It took me many years of debunking myths I had been taught through my family, society, religion and even friends. What I have found to be true is that people generally do not mean you harm when they impose their beliefs on you. After all, that is their beliefs and they know them to be true for them. But remember they are true for them and need not be true for you.

For example, in my father's era, it was quite common, even encouraged, to stick with one company all your life. Today, however, you are told something quite different. In fact, a year ago, a respected business contact of mine told me to not stick at one job for more than 5 years. Again, this is her belief system, but it is far from my father's belief.

You need to take ownership of your own belief system and find what is true for you. A simple question to ask yourself is how does someone's opinion make you feel? If you agree with them, great. If not, don't judge them for what they think, just find what holds true for you and stick with that.

Your belief system can change over the years, so it is good to check in with yourself from time to time, and re-evaluate where you stand on your beliefs. There is nothing wrong with changing your beliefs at any point in your life.

So how do you change your thinking? Simply put, you cannot change something if you don't know what you are changing. So to begin with, start noticing the thoughts you are having. How do they make you feel? Do they constrict you or empower you? Do they make you feel heavy or light, happy or sad?

Don't be hard on yourself when you notice that you think erroneous and destructive thoughts and find it difficult to stop them. It is not about stopping these thoughts. It is about noticing them, not placing any emotion to them and letting them just drift on by.

One of the best analogies I can give you to help you with this, is as follows:

1. see yourself as the big blue clear sky
2. see your thoughts as the clouds drifting on by
3. some clouds are light and fluffy whilst others are dark and heavy
4. don't place any judgement on the clouds, they are just clouds
5. see them come into view and then watch as they float on by

The secret here is not to attach any emotions to any of your thoughts. Just see them for what they are. They are not your enemy.

You need to learn to make them your allies.

For every negative thought you find yourself having, counterbalance this by repeating the exact opposite of what you were thinking.

For example, if you were thinking 'I am useless', replace this with *'I am capable and able to do whatever I put my mind to'*. Repeat this a few times, until you start feeling like this is your reality. It might feel contrived at first, but after a while you will start to think, *'of course I am more than capable!'* You will even begin to wonder why you ever thought some of those negative thoughts in the first place.

A sure way of noticing your thoughts is to notice what you say. Words were once thoughts and your words become actions. So it is important to change your thinking, as your thoughts have a direct influence on your behaviour.

If you have someone who is going through this process with you, you could be *12 Steps to Loving You Buddies*. Someone that you can rely on to be gentle and patient with you. This can be someone that you trust with your innermost secrets and someone who will give you honest and constructive feedback.

A word of caution, always thank someone for their opinion, but do not take it on as the truth until you have gone within to see if you agree with the sentiments expressed.

By changing your thinking, you are empowering you to be the best version of you that you can possibly be.

I am not asking you to be unrealistic in your own self-assessment, but rather to look at your thoughts with sober judgement, and to learn to discern the thoughts that weigh you down from the ones that lighten your being.

Choose the thoughts that lighten your being, always.

YOU AND YOUR THOUGHTS

1. Watch your thoughts over the next few days? Are you aware just how habitual your thinking has become? What can you do to become more aware of your thinking patterns?

2. What are the thoughts you think about yourself? Are they positive or negative thoughts?

3. What are the thoughts you think about your job? Are they positive or negative, and if negative, what could you change your thoughts to be?

4. What thoughts do you think about current relationships in your life? Do they tear the relationship/s down or build

them up? How can you reframe your thoughts to more positive ones?

5. What beliefs do you have around:
   a) Yourself
   b) Love
   c) Life
   d) Your finances
   e) Your career
   f) Your relationships
   g) Your partner
   h) Your family

Are these beliefs destructive or empowering, and if destructive, how can you change your beliefs to being more positive and liberating?

6. On a scale of 1 – 10 how would you describe your current thought patterns? 1 being extremely negative and pessimistic and 10 being completely liberating and

empowering. How can you change your thinking to reach 10 on this scale?

7. Is it possible for you to change your current thinking patterns? What is keeping you stuck in your old ways?

AFFIRMATION FOR CHAPTER 4

I change my habitual thought-patterns easily and effortlessly. I only think thoughts that are for my higher good.

PHASE II

ALL ABOUT CHANGE

CHAPTER 5

HEALING THE HURT

What you hide can hurt you.

(Deborah King)

It is not so much the healing of the hurt that needs focused attention, but rather the stripping away of the layers of hurt that has accumulated over the years.

This will help you find your true inner core of Love and Joy. This will be a coming back to our true selves, the essence of who we are.

In the words of the late Dr. Wayne Dyer – *don't ask to be healed; ask to be restored to that perfection from which you emanated.*

When I found myself going back in time and facing the hurt that had stock-piled in the dark warehouse of my mind, I found an analogy that helped me learn just how to let go of the grievances I held for so long And you can do this too.

I imagined my hurt as barnacles clinging to my soul. They clung securely to me and refused to budge no matter how hard I tried to pry the hurt from my emotional body.

Have you ever tried to pry a barnacle from a rock? If so, what was your experience?

If you have ever tried to pry barnacles from a rock you will know that if you touch it ever so gently it will wiggle a bit, but the moment you place pressure on it to rip it from the rock, it instinctively grips to the surface and remains firmly attached to the rock.

This is how I felt when I was doing the healing work. The key here is to be gentle with yourself and know that you are a loving being, deserving of all the Love and happiness that this world has to offer.

Here is an exercise for you to practice when dealing with releasing the hurt in your life.

Imagine you have a dark warehouse in the back of your mind and in this room you stock-pile all the hurt, betrayals, rejection, loneliness, abandonment, fear, guilt, shame, scarcity, anxiety, depression, worry and all the other negative situations that have played out in your life up until now.

Imagine that you have a broom to take with you into the warehouse so that you can clear out the space, thus giving you space to put all the Love, Joy, peace, happiness, wealth, prosperity, abundance, success, kindness, gentleness, patience and so many other life-affirming experiences into it.

You enter the warehouse, and it is shrouded in darkness. You are apprehensive about approaching this space, as you have not been in here for some time and you do not know what you will find.

You remember that no matter what has happened to you in the past, it can no longer hurt or hold power over you. You have the choice to give your power away or to keep your power and you take a firm stand and declare that you will no longer give your power away to anyone. You take ownership of your life. It is time to clear out the warehouse.

As you go in, your eyes begin to adjust to the darkness surrounding you. You walk over to the wall, and turn on the switch. You notice a large table in the middle of the room with a whole lot of boxes on it.

You walk over to the table and notice that the boxes are labelled and filed in alphabetical order. Some of the boxes have names on them and others have dates.

You pull up a chair, and let the broom lean against the table. Undecided as to whether or not to open the boxes, you decide to look inside each box and to finally forgive those who played a part in hurting you. As if by some magical force, the moment you make this decision, rose-tinted glasses float down from above.

You reach out and place them on the bridge of your nose and you know it is safe to look at your life's hurt with these rose-tinted glasses, as it will block the intensity of the negative emotions you once felt.

You will see what is in each box, and then you will be able to make a conscious decision to let go of the grievances (hurt) and to send Love, light and blessing where once the hurt had been.

One by one you begin to open the boxes. You are amazed at some of the things you find there, as they now appear to you as being petty. But you remember that at the time, those things really hurt you.

As you open each box and go through the hurt, you silently say a prayer of thanks and gratitude for lessons learnt, you send Love, light and blessings to all parties involved in the hurt, and you put the lid back on the box and place the completed ones to one side. This takes you some time, and you decide not to go through them all at once.

You get up and take the broom and boxes you have already cleared and you leave the room, knowing that tomorrow you are going to come back and continue with the clearing of the space until all the boxes have been removed.

Once you have left the warehouse, you go to the open field outside, and you place the completed boxes in a barrel. You take some wood, newspaper and firelighters and set the contents on fire.

You know that with the burning of the boxes, you are releasing all the hurt that once was and you are healed instantaneously, at a very deep cellular level.

You have released those who have hurt you and you have set yourself free from the bondage these hurts once caused you.

You consciously make the decision that as and when these situations arise in the future, that you will no longer be storing them in boxes in the warehouse but you will deal with these grievances as and when they arise.

You will look at them, learn from them, forgive where forgiveness is required, and you will let them go in exactly the same way that you let the negative thought clouds float on by.

Hurt comes in many guises. What might seem a small hurt to someone might seem big to you. The only true way to heal your hurt is to show up honestly when dealing with them. Hold no judgement towards the hurt or other parties involved in doing the hurting, just show up with the intention to heal and release yourself from the hurt that once caused you so much pain. Acknowledge your feelings and don't belittle them. If someone hurt you intentionally or unintentionally, you still sit with the hurt. Remember when people hurt you, it says more about them than it does about you. When someone attacks you personally, know that it is their problem and not yours. They are seeing themselves in you and it is far easier to lash out at someone else than it is to acknowledge their own shortcomings.

'You are the work of God, and His work is wholly lovable and wholly loving. This is how you must think of yourself in your heart, because that is what you are.' – A Course in Miracles

Healing from your hurt is a Love Story you give yourself. You are showing yourself the ultimate gift of kindness.

You are setting yourself free from all the hurt you once had buried deep inside. And you are releasing yourself and others from the scars that these situations once caused.

Once you have completed this process a few times, you will notice that you are not exempt from being hurt again. This is human nature. To feel pain is tough and uncomfortable. Sometimes the pain seems so unbearable, but you will grow in strength each time you release the grievances you hold towards yourself and others.

Your most important Love Story is the one you hold with yourself. In your heart lies the key to your eternal happiness. For you to truly love someone else, you first need to love yourself. This is why so many relationships do not work. We try and replace self-love with the love of another. This is just simply not possible. You are perfect just as you are, scars and all. You are doing the best you can with what you have, and for today, that is enough.

So many people fill the void of a lack of self-love with materialism or relationships that block them having to face their own realities. Ask yourself this, if I was not in this relationship, would I be comfortable in my own presence? If you answer no, then you know it is time to go within and so some serious soul-searching healing inner work.

It is important to discuss discrimination and false beliefs.

Growing up on the coast meant that from a very young age I was aware of the shape and size of my body, and of the bodies around me. I was what you would call a 'lanky' kid. I was tall and slender, and had a runner's physique. I used to play volleyball on the beach and was a very active teenager. I was very self-conscious when going to the beach, even though I had no reason to be. This was the pressure that society had placed on me through advertising, the ideal model look, the image that I thought boys liked. These things were really important to me then, and whilst I now like a well-toned physique, it is for me and not some dictated story born from someone else.

Although I had a relationship with God starting from a very young age and although this relationship has stood through the test of time, I still had not come to see some of the misconceptions I had learnt along the way. I knew nothing about a God who did not care how I looked. I just thought I had to be pretty and beautiful on the outside, to be acceptable. I knew nothing about the beauty from within, not until I was older and wiser.

Like so many now say; if I knew then what I know now, I would not have treated myself so harshly. I would have been far gentler on myself and those around me.

I held myself to such high standards, and all in the name of being loved.

I did not see the truth that I was lovable exactly as I was.

I understand why some teenagers battle with their self-identity, because peer pressure is truly at its peak at this stage in your life. The older you get, the things you once held dear, no longer hold meaning for you. For example, the qualities I once wanted in a man are now no longer the qualities I want.

If I can give you one gift when it comes to loving yourself, it is this – *find your meaning in life, and pursue that*. All else will fall into place. Do not shy away from your own truth but rather own who you are and make a conscious decision to love yourself from this day forward.

Loving yourself ensures you set healthy boundaries. It allows your no to be 'no' and your yes to be 'yes', and it gives you an inner peace which transcends all understanding. When you have a *coming back to yourself a-ha moment*, you realise that you are more beautiful than you imagined. True beauty comes from within and radiates outwards and you are truly beautiful.

My heart reaches out to those who have body image challenges; when you see yourself as too fat or too thin, too fair-skinned or too dark and when being just who you are is not enough. Your hair is too long or too short, and the colour is just not right.

You shy away from the grey hairs, and rush out to buy that perfection in a box, and you hide the grey away from yourself and others.

You strive to change.

You eat a disproportionate diet and this does not nourish your body sufficiently and you work out at the gym for hours at a time. Now, there is nothing wrong with having a healthy balance of exercise and eating correctly, but everything in moderation.

I was once this person and I am now dedicated to making healthy choices when it comes to what I eat and the exercise I do. I have started doing yoga and am amazed at just how much I have let my body and fitness levels drop over the years. No matter what the excuse, I did this to myself. No-one forced me to sit on the couch and binge-watch my favourite television series instead of doing exercise. I was full of excuses and the main one was that I was exhausted after coming home from a stressful job. Now although this was true, what I really needed was to get off the couch and go and do some exercise, and this would have helped combat my fatigue. I knew this at the time to be true, so I honestly have no excuse.

I knew there was an underlying issue why I allowed my weight to fluctuate like it has over the years. So I did the inner work and found the following. When I was younger, fit and pretty, I saw how I allowed myself to be manipulated by wrongful relationships with men. The thought that men only wanted for me for sex was planted in my brain. I decided not to be a victim of this again, so I let myself go.

I wanted to be loved for me and not for what I looked like, and this belief became my relationship downfall for many years.

Based on this wrongful thinking, I allowed myself to lessen my self-care. I have since learnt that we are never too old to learn and make different choices in our lives that will allow us to live healthier and more rewarding lives.

Now here is a shocker. Do you know that half the time we get hurt, those things that hurt us either never happened or we misperceived a situation?

Recently I thought I had upset a friend. I allowed this guilt, fear and sadness to become all-consuming and needless to say that the next few days were truly tormented. It consumed my thoughts and I found it hard to even think of sitting down to write anything. It was only when I asked my friend if I had upset her in any way, and she said absolutely not, that I realised just how much value we place on things that are not even true. Tears were shed, my heart was heavy and time was wasted on something that was not real. So how do we go from allowing ourselves to sit in hurt, whether real or unreal, before we face the hurt and move on with our lives? Sitting with hurt for too long is truly is a waste of precious energy and time.

A Course in Miracles talks about time being created so that we have the necessary space to learn lessons on earth.

This is why you shouldn't waste time. I told you before that time would cease when it was no longer useful as a learning aid – A Course in Miracles.

Now whilst hurt is a valuable teacher, I would much rather be spending my time learning how to co-create my life than spending it on feeling pain. The lesson for me is to learn to let go of grievances as and when they arise.

Healing and releasing past hurt is a conscious decision, one that must not be made lightly, because once you begin this journey all sorts of things will come to the surface that you might not have thought of in years. It is important to hold yourself in a space of forgiveness and to be gentle with yourself when doing the inner work. You are not the first person to be hurt and you will not be the last. Everyone faces hurt at some time in their lives; it is how you deal with the hurt that will set you apart from all the rest.

What I want to end this chapter off with is by reminding you that we are all connected. What we do to others, we do to ourselves, so when you forgive another, you are also forgiving yourself.

We are not separate in this universe and we are all one in this great tapestry of life. For every grievance you release, you allow space for Love, Joy and kindness to shine through. So be the light that you are and let your light shine to everyone through your forgiveness.

Releasing the hurt does not mean that you condone the behaviour it simply means that you are no longer willing to let the hurt rob you of your Joy.

There is a wonderful tradition in Japan.

When something is broken, e.g. a bowl, it is fixed with gold, so that the once whole object is now whole again, but this time it has gold lines where the cracks once were. It is still an object of beauty. The same is with us and our hurts.

When we heal our hurts and let go of our grievances, our beauty continues to shine through, and we are stronger than we once were.

Healing your hurts and releasing your grievances is a necessity for walking the path of truly loving yourself. You owe it to yourself to be kind and gentle when dealing with your past. Forgive yourself and others. It will set you all free.

HEALING YOUR HURT & RELEASING YOUR GRIEVANCES

1. Can you think of anyone you need to forgive who has hurt you in the past? Are you willing to let the resentment and hurt go, or do you want to hold on to it a bit longer? What purpose would that serve?

2. Look at your life in a horizontal timeline, from birth to where you are today. Map out important stages in your life where you were let down, such as if your parents got divorced, a serious breakup, and a trauma suffered. Look at

each situation separately and silently send Love and forgiveness to all involved. Remember, you are not condoning the action; you are just no longer going to allow these situations to rob you of your Joy.

3. Perhaps one of the most difficult situations to face is the one where you have to forgive yourself for all sorts of things. Make a list of where you have let yourself down, and then address each one separately. Know that at the time you were doing the best you can with the resources you had. Show yourself compassion and Love.

4. Healing the child within. Wherever you are at in your life right now, know that there is a young version of yourself that needs Love and compassion. Imagine yourself sitting on a beach by the sea-side with your younger self. What would you tell your younger self about the life lessons you have learnt?

5. It is not always easy or possible to ask people to release you from the pain you might have caused them, so instead, go within and send them a silent prayer of release and ask

their higher selves to release you from any harm you might have intentionally or unintentionally caused them.

6. Commit to dealing with grievances as and when they arise and don't go to bed with anger in your heart. Can you do this? If not, why not?
7. Write all your past grievances in a journal and then once you have completed this, burn the journal as a reference that the past hurts and grievances are released from your life.

AFFIRMATION FOR CHAPTER 5

I let go of all hurts and grievances and replace them with Love.

CHAPTER 6
GROUNDING TOOLS FOR YOUR JOURNEY

When we expand our thinking and beliefs, our love flows freely. When we contract, we shut ourselves off.

(Louise Hay)

There are many tools for you to choose from that can help keep you balanced and grounded. Without the appropriate tools and techniques, you will find yourself tossed back and forth as you try to navigate through life.

In this fast-paced life we all need some way of remaining calm and centred and balanced in our lives. We need to have tools in our toolbox to help us remain balanced and grounded, regardless of the circumstances we face every day.

Your life is constantly on the go as you try to juggle your career, time for your family and friends and time for yourself. Burn out is a possibility, unless you take serious action to combat this.

Over the years I have accumulated a variety of tools that have helped me remain balanced and grounded. I have exercised, meditated, practiced Reiki and Chakra Cleansing and Balancing,

I delved into the angelic realm, shamanism and practiced the art of visualisation, I trained and qualified in Neuro Linguistic Programming and practiced watching my breath in stressful situations. I started yoga.

My toolbox is ever expanding and these are just a few of the tools I have used. What works for me does not necessarily mean they will work for you. I am forever adding and subtracting tools from my toolbox.

You need to be open to the tools that resonate with you. If you knew what these tools were, what would they look like to you? It will help if you sit quietly and ask yourself what it is that you need, to be able to maintain your balance in stressful situations?

Imagine yourself in the workplace or at home, and a stressful situation occurs. Your printer won't work and you urgently need reports for a meeting that is starting in 5 minutes. Or your oven has packed up and you have guests arriving in a few hours for dinner.

Have you found that when one thing goes wrong, a domino of ill-fated events seems to occur one after the other? You would not be the first person to experience this, and it seems that the reason for this is quite simple.

When you experience stress you emit a stress frequency and you thus act as a magnet for other stressful events to occur. The secret is to stop the stress at source and not allow it to wreak more unnecessary havoc in your life.

Perhaps painting or playing a musical instrument helps you feel balanced and grounded. Listening to soothing music or taking walks in nature can also help. I find that sitting by the ocean and watching the ebb and flow of the tide has an immense soothing effect on my soul. When I am faced with immediate stress, however, I cannot just go and sit by the ocean, so I keep nature sound CDs in my car. I can then responsibly go off on a seaside adventure without actually being there.

How do you get to choose the tools that best help you remain grounded? You take a journey within and through trial and error you will find the ones that help you the best. Some tools can be used over a lengthier period of time than others. For example, in a crisis situation you will want a tool that works really fast. For moments such as this, I created a trigger using the art of visualisation that helps me to calm down instantaneously.

Let me give you an example of how to apply this in your own life. Sit quietly and press your thumb and middle finger together. While you do this, imagine your breathing slowing down. Imagine the sounds of seagulls flying above, or birds chirping in the trees.

You can image anything pleasant while you are pressing your thumb and middle finger together. Hold this position and continue to imagine soothing sounds and picture being out in nature. Continue to do this for at least 3 – 5 minutes.

Then slowly release your thumb and middle finger. Do this a few times each day.

Now the fun begins. When a stressful situation occurs, immediately press your thumb and middle finger together, and you should start having the same soothing sensations you experienced when you were doing the exercise above. If you don't feel this immediately, don't stress. Just go back to practising this technique and eventually your sub-conscious will see this practice as a trigger for calmness and slowing down.

This works for me every time and it is really helpful when you find yourself in a meeting or having a difficult conversation with someone and you do not have the opportunity to just walk out and leave the room. I press my thumb and middle finger together, and I am reminded that all is well in my world, my breathing slows down and I am once again in control of my wellbeing.

Affirmations are also a good way to centre yourself. Affirmations, much like mantras, are short sentences repeated over and over again, until you start to feel a shift within yourself that starts to believe the words you are saying.

In the words of a song sung by Julie Andrews – *let's start at the very beginning, a very good place to start, when you read you begin with ABC, when you sing you begin with doh reh me ....* (from The Sound of Music).

In the beginning ....

Your morning practice sets your intention for the day. If you do not have a morning practice, now is as good a time as any to start your day off on the right footing.

My practice is simple. I get up and sit on the edge of my bed. With gratitude in my heart, I say thank you for another opportunity to serve others. I spend time in quiet contemplation, gratitude and prayer and then I read some inspiring literature. Currently I am reading A Course in Miracles, and a while back I read The Tao Te Ching. You might get inspiration from other books. Remember to remain authentic to your own personal likes and dislikes. There is no right and wrong choice, the key here is to find reading that uplifts you to embrace the day with open arms and not stooped shoulders and a hunched back. It is important to me that my heart chakra be open and clear for the day ahead.

Throughout the day I check in with myself to see how I am feeling. I do a quick scan over and within my body and I isolate where accumulated stress is showing up. If I have tension in my shoulders, I squeeze my shoulder blades together, hold for a short while and then release.

If I sense a headache coming on, I adjust the brightness on my computer screen (my practical side shining through) and I rub the sides of my temples to bring relief. I focus on what could be causing the stress and I envision the stress as a cloud, drifting in and out of my awareness.

I just let it go.

And I also press my thumb and middle finger together to remind me that all is well in my world.

When something stressful is happening in the workplace, I see the troubles that I face as clouds in the sky, drifting in and out of view. If the problem is a person being hostile or angry, I visualise them being gifted with softness and an incredible lightness of being. I see the anger evaporate from their shoulders, like steam off a hot road after a sudden cloud burst. I send them Love and peace, all the while keeping my composure and balance. *The softest of all things overrides the hardest of all things – Tao Te Ching (43rd verse).*

The key to being able to do this is to remain acutely aware of what is happening around you.

Grounding tools for using in the workplace is really important, especially if you have a very stressful job.

It is not always possible to meditate when at work, but you can go to the one place where you won't be disturbed (hopefully) for a few minutes, and that is the bathroom. Then just practice visualising the situation turning out for the best for all parties.

In the evening, make a conscious decision before you go to bed at night to see a playback of your day and forgive grievances where forgiveness is required. I wish someone had told me about this years ago. It would have saved me much heartache and unnecessary hurt. Before you go to sleep, say thank you for the day you have had and ask for a peaceful night's rest.

Here are some grounding tools for you to consider, in no particular order:

1. expressing gratitude for all you have
2. taking walks in nature
3. sitting by the ocean
4. doing exercise
5. meditating
6. reiki (or any other healing modality)
7. chakra cleansing and balancing
8. listening to soothing music
9. painting
10. writing in your journal
11. helping others through charity work
12. yoga

This list could go on for pages, but these are just a few ideas to get you thinking about what could work for you.

The Tao does nothing,
but leaves nothing undone.

If powerful men
could centre themselves in it,
the whole world would be transformed

by itself, in its natural rhythms.

When life is simple,
pretenses fall away;
our essential natures shine through.

By not wanting, there is calm,
and the world will straighten itself.
When there is silence,
one finds the anchor of the universe within oneself.
(The Tao Te Ching – 37th verse)

GROUNDING TOOLS FOR YOUR JOURNEY

1. How stressful is your current lifestyle and what current activities do you do to combat this stress?

2. How balanced is your life right now? How much time do you spend daily (in hours), doing the following:
    a. Spiritual practice   _____
    b. Physical practice   _____
    c. On social media   _____
    d. With family   _____

e.	With friends	_____
f.	At work / school	_____
g.	At play	_____
h.	Sleeping	_____

3. Based on the above, where can you re-adjust your schedule to create a more balanced life?

4. Which of the following grounding tools resonate with you?
   a. Exercise – Gym
   b. Exercise – Running
   c. Exercise – Walking
   d. Exercise – Swimming
   e. Exercise – Cycling
   f. Corrective eating
   g. Reiki
   h. Chakra Cleansing and Balancing
   i. Acupuncture
   j. Meditation
   k. Yoga
   l. Other: _____

5. Based on the above, what can you do to find out more about the tools that resonate with you, and when can you start implementing this healthy life change?

AFFIRMATION FOR CHAPTER 6

I have all the resources I need to live a fully actualised and balanced life.

CHAPTER 7
SOULFUL INTEGRATIONS

Look at all the parts of you
That makes up who you are
Individually they are their own
Together you are One with God
(Jennifer L. Breakey)

We are a multifaceted species. People say we complicate life and that life is actually quite simple, but the truth is that life *is* complicated. There is so much choice. Which path do we take? What career should I choose? Should I change jobs? Should I work on this relationship or has it passed its expiry date?

Even if we go within to find our inner GPS, we need to be certain that what we are hearing is in fact the right way for us to go. And it is okay to be a complicated individual.

You can still have peace within the confines of your complexity. Peace is coming to a place within yourself that you can call home; where what you think, say, do, and who you are, are all one and the same.

In this chapter we focus on the Soulful Integrations of your mind, body and spirit.

We also look at integrating your physical, mental, emotional and spiritual bodies, and then we look at authentically integrating who you are in the workplace.

When I was young, I battled with the concept of the Holy Trinity. This integration of 3 into 1 was baffling for a child's mind. The best way to explain this to myself was to think of an egg. There is the egg shell, the egg yolk and the egg white. All three of them are separate, yet together they are the egg. And so it is with the Holy Trinity. God, Jesus Christ and the Holy Spirit are all individual facets of God, and being individual facets, they are also integrated and are one with God, as God.

If you find the concept of your mind, body and spirit to be too esoteric or pie-in-the-sky for you, then think of it like this. Your mind is the way you think, the place where you hold your beliefs, and we have already seen that your thoughts have a direct impact on the wellbeing of your body. So an integration/connection between the two already exists. Your spirit is the Spark of the Divine that you are. You came from Source, and you can only be a part of that from whence you came. Our body is the vessel that houses our spirit, and again, there is the integration between the two.

This exercise should help you ease into the understanding of the integration of your mind, body and spirit.

Find a place where you can sit quietly for about half an hour without being interrupted.

Sit quietly and close your eyes. Become aware of your breathing, inhaling peace and exhaling stress and confusion. See peace enter you with every breath you take and see the stress and confusion leave your body as you exhale. Do this at least 10 times, slowly and consciously. Breathe in …. Breathe out ….

Once you get to that calm space within, notice your thoughts. Do not judge or fight them; that would be futile. Just see them floating in as clouds and then see them floating on by out of your view. Attach no emotions or feelings to any of these thoughts.

Let go of all the stress you are experiencing and slowly loosen and relax all the muscles in your body. Now in your mind's eye, see your mind, your body and your spirit as separate entities. Acknowledge your mind, body and spirit. Now see them as separate and then slowly bring them together until they are merged as one, as you. You are not just your mind, body, or spirit. You are all three as one, mirroring the Trinity.

Meditation and visualisation are excellent tools to help with your soulful integrations. As discussed, life can be simple or complexed. It really is all just a matter of perception.

You might have heard people talk about our physical, mental, emotional and spiritual bodies, as though they are a few bodies in one.

1. Physical – your body
2. Mental – your mind
3. Emotional – your emotions

4.   Spiritual – your spirituality

In truth, we see one body with the physical eye. And some people live from the premise that this is all we are. A human body, having a human experience on earth and when it is all over we turn to dust, and as they say – lights out, show is over, there is no more.

On the other hand, there is a vast majority who believe that this simply cannot be true, either through their own experience or having learnt about an experience from someone else.

Think of a delicious warm Irish stew. The ingredients for this stew are carrots, potatoes, peas, onion, stock, meat, garlic and oil. Once the stew is made, we prepare rice and sit down to eat a deliciously wholesome meal. So, what is the stew? It is the accumulation of all the ingredients in the pot, cooked and served hot on a bed of rice. The carrot is still the carrot and the potato still the potato. But together they make up the stew. The stew is still the culmination of all the various ingredients, but the ingredients still hold their own identify.

Now think of you in the same way – many ingredients make up who you are. Your body, mind, emotions and spirit are all a part of what makes you who you are. It is from this basis that we look at the integration of all these facets that create you.

Every area of you is so intricately linked. When one area of your life suffers it spills over into other areas of your life.

For example, if you are feeling emotionally exhausted, what other areas in your life are feeling the same way?

One can even break your life into other areas, such as:

1. Your career (your calling, purpose, mission in life)
2. Your health (physical, mental & emotional wellbeing)
3. Your wealth (prosperity and abundance thinking)
4. Your spiritual practice (your very own long walk to freedom)

There are other areas, but the ones listed above are the major ones.

It helps to look for patterns in your life. When you deal with the root issue, all areas are corrected at the same time, just like a ripple effect. One area mirrors the other, but instead of separating ourselves, by calling each part a different area, we need to see ourselves as one being.

To integrate who we are, we need to love each and every aspect of ourselves. It would be reckless and unhealthy to see the areas in ourselves as separate from each other. We are not just our body, we are not just our thoughts and we are only just spirit when we transition from this world.

When we see ourselves as lovable, for that is what we truly are, love will rush in and begin the healing process.

We need to send love to all the areas within us, and not pay too much attention to one area and not the other.

This is where imbalance occurs.

For example, if I focus more on my body and getting fit, but ignore my emotional wellbeing, my emotions will be given free-reign to run havoc in my life. So it is important to pay equal attention to all areas in your life. There will be times when one area requires extra special attention, for example a health issue that might come to the surface, and this is okay. So long as the other areas remain in check.

When I ask myself 'who am I', you know, the actual 'I' part of me, I come to the realisation that I am all these things and none of these things. Such is the dichotomy of Life.

I am my all-encompassing Self, and then, I am none of this. Science has proven that time does not exist. And, if time does not exist, am I truly here in the here and now?

According to A Course in Miracles, time is a construct whose sole purpose is to provide the space for us to be able to learn lessons. When we no longer need to learn, time will cease.

Not so long ago I had an interesting conversation with my father, who is a respected and knowledgeable man.

He has spent the greater part of his life always studying something, from physics to calculus to French, and so much more.

His study is full of books covering philosophy, physics and other literature, and he acquired 3 degrees in his lifetime.

One day we were discussing life after death. After losing his wife, my step-mother, a few years back, his need for reassurance that he will be with her again one day was raw and palpable. They were married for over 40 years and were best of friends.

He pondered how could all the souls that have been on earth fit into a heaven and a hell. (I personally do not believe in two separate places known as heaven and hell. I believe heaven and hell is here and now, and we get to choose which one we live in – Love or Fear.)

Thanks to Anita Moorjani's book Dying to Be Me, for sharing her experience of what the realm is like, the one where we 'go' after death.

My father's question seemed out of place. Here is a man who is well-versed in the bible and physics, so surely he should know, even if from a scientific perspective, the answer to this.

Over and above this, if you just look at planet earth in relation to the universe (or should that now be called multiverse?), we will see that earth is but a speck of dust in the greater scheme of things.

The earth is ever-expanding and this can seem incomprehensible, so how much more is the thought of other dimensions incomprehensible? When we are driven by fear, everything that once seemingly made sense in our lives suddenly loses its grip on our sense of reality and this shakes the very foundation on which we base our beliefs.

My answer was simple. 'Dad', I said. 'Remember one of Albert Einstein's quotes – *whereas human intelligence is limited, human stupidity is not?*' We both chuckled, as he knew I was taken a well-meaning knock at his question. I continued. 'Think about eternity. If eternity if infinitum, and if we live in a universe that is ever-expanding, and if eternity has no beginning and no end, is it not possible that we as mere mortals cannot begin to fathom that no space exists in the other realm? And as such, all souls will take up no space but just be together, bound neither by space or time?' Again, Anita Moorjani describes this picture perfectly.

We both thought about that for a while and agreed that this was possible. I hoped that my answer would give my dad the solace he needs to know with certainty that he and my step-mom would indeed be together again one day.

Sometimes we want to take away someone else's pain, but all we can do is sit with them and hold a gentle space of loving kindness and compassion, as no words can help alleviate what they are feeling. With my father being such a rational and logical thinker, I hoped that my words would bring some form of truth to his heart.

Now I know this might sound odd, but here is something that I battled with for so many years and I knew that if I was to experience true Love and Joy in my life, then I needed to show up authentically wherever I find myself.

And, the workplace was a great way to begin. And here is what happened when I opened myself up to this possibility.

Some years back, holding a senior management position in a large manufacturing company, I knew that we lacked in certain areas, and one of these areas was in the development of the senior management team. Each one of us was gifted and talented in our respective roles, but when it came to emotional intelligence, or putting aside our differences and opinions to best serve the greater good of the company, this was a daily battle. Egos would flare up; people would not be supportive of one another and generally just moan and groan about how they had to save the day because no-one else would. Either I was going to be a part of the solution to this or I was going to land up leaving the company. I acknowledged that training and development was a part of my portfolio, so I need to make this happen.

After giving this much thought, I decided to illicit the help of a professional trainer with whom I had worked before, and who had a way of bringing the exact change that was required. The entire senior management team went on what I would like to call – a *soulful excursion*. And for a while, this training helped.

It was interesting to see the dynamics of different people at play. Some were really keen to get stuck in and do the work, and others thought that EQ and the likes was for the fairies.

Before long, things went back to the way they were. The 'sandwich approach' was soon forgotten, egos started flaring up again, and what was once an opportunity for tremendous change, growth and great learnings, soon became the derelict team it once was. And this was very hard for me to see. In so many ways our team was dynamic and productive, but in other ways, there was still so much room for growth.

At work, it is so important to see past the bottom line and to stay objective and hold no judgements. As humans, we are prone to errors, but it is in the releasing of these, taking accountability of our role to play in the workplace, that we see things start to change for the better.

I had to ask myself how I could possibly show up at work each day, when I seemed to be awakened and everyone else seemed to be asleep. And then I got it. I finally got it. All the external situations were nothing but a reflection of my inner workings. Where was I acting like this to myself?

I most certainly was not showing up with compassion, love and support to the team. Instead, I showed up with judgement, criticism, and anger. As hard as that was for me to face, that is how I felt and it took me about 12 months to work this all out of my system.

Something had to change, and that something turned to be somebody and that somebody turned out to be me.

I had to change. And this was difficult, because the externals had not changed, but I had to change regardless.

And I did. It was not before long that I started sensing a shift. A very uncomfortable shift. You know, the kind of shift that happens when you realise that your old familiar pair of sneakers no longer fits you comfortably and they have worn down beyond repair. I had outgrown my job and it was time to make a move.

The interesting part of my career is that I have always prayed before I went to work at a new company. I would ask the Universe where I should work. Where was I needed the most? Sometimes it wasn't so much where I was needed, but was what I needed at the time. Lessons were learnt. Tears were shed, but we keep on moving.

Instead of making a decision, I decided to go and see a psychologist to help me see if I was making this decision based on my fears or if I was coming from a space of growing and self-development, and finally allowing myself the opportunity to live the life of my dreams. Going to see a professional helped me with my own journey of going within. I wanted only an objective view of a very subjective decision I had to make.

I was pleasantly surprised to see my intentions were on path with my own created destiny, and so I decided to quit.

I gave up a senior management position in a large corporation (2nd largest in the world of its kind) to follow through on a promise I had made to God so many years ago.

And that promise was to bring 12 Steps to Loving You to the world. This would not have been a possible reality, had I not authentically shown up in my workplace.

If you want to authentically show up in your workplace, you need to be the one who needs to be willing to change. Every situation that is happening outside of you, ask yourself this – how am I treating myself internally? Are you showing up with compassion, love and service or are you being judgemental, critical and a part of the problem? I was once part of the problem and now I am proof that you can change.

Do not be hard on yourself but rather show yourself the love, kindness and gentleness you deserve. Although it took me about a year to forgive the situations I had experienced in the workplace, forgive I did, and I am grateful for these lessons. When I think of those who let me down, who betrayed me and who hurt me, I sent them love, light, blessings and happiness for all eternity. So much time is spent at the workplace; why not make it a fun and loving place to work. Set the intention, hold the vision and walk your talk.

YOUR QUEST TO SOULFUL INTEGRATIONS

1. How easy is it for you to show up authentically in the workplace?

2. What challenges do you have in the workplace that stops you being your authentic self?

3. How can you overcome these challenges? List the actionable steps that you can take to overcome these challenges.

4. What choices do you have if you are not able to show up authentically in your workplace? List at least 3 choices.

5. What are your current energy levels like in your life? Are they the same in all areas? (E.g. depleted energy / depleted finances? – look for the patterns.)

6. Do the mind, body, spirit exercise mentioned earlier in this chapter. How did this exercise make you feel? Do you feel that all areas of your life are integrated?

7. What is the fun ratio in your life? How can you bring more fun-filled experiences into your daily activities?

8. Are you able to own your own identity without being pressured by your family, friends or colleagues?

9. What practices can you do, such as meditation, yoga, visualisation, to help integrate Soulful Integrations into your daily routine?

AFFIRMATION FOR CHAPTER 7

I joyously integrate all aspects of my life.

CHAPTER 8

SOULFUL CREATIONS

Don't die with your music still inside you.
(Dr. Wayne W. Dyer)

Up until this point, you have learnt:
1. that everything is energy
2. all about your true magnificence
3. how to show up as your authentic self
4. that changing your thinking can radically change your life
5. how to let go of and heal past hurts/grievances
6. about grounding tools to help you stay balanced
7. how to integrate all facets of who you are into the Oneness that you are

You are now about to learn how to be the creator of your own life. If this doesn't excite you, I don't know what will. We have the power to create absolutely whatever we desire. So let's learn from the best and get the original blueprint of life.

Creation happens and follows our thoughts. You can create absolutely anything – true story. So what then keeps us from doing this? Is it fear that holds us back? Or is it that you feel unworthy of receiving all the goodness this life has to offer?

Do you have a belief that everyone else gets the great things, but not you?

Do you shy away from your own magnificence? You are such a radiant light – people need to see you and hear you. You are important to others. You are important to me. You need to be important to yourself.

If creating our best life was that simple, would we not all have wonder-filled lives. Would we not all be creating masterpieces? Would we not have the desires of our hearts? Some achieve this, others don't. Why is that? Are some born with the silver spoon in their mouth? Or is it random luck, fate or just some coincidence that their lives seemed to fall into perfect unison with their desires and dreams?

I can answer this question, but you might not hear me. So I ask that you keep an open heart and an open mind and allow any and all possibilities to be the possibilities that could create the opportunities for you to live the life of your dreams.

As I sit here writing this chapter, I am reminded of the movie and book *The Diving Bell and the Butterfly*. It is a true story about Jean-Dominique Bauby, who had a massive stroke when he was 42 years old which resulted in him being in a coma for 3 weeks and then he had locked-in syndrome for a year, before he passed on when he was only 43 years old.

He was the editor of the Elle magazine and was in every sense of the word, truly successful in his career.

Insomuch as this book is a tragedy, it is also a book about the strength of the human spirit.

Jean-Do, as he was called by his friends, wrote his book by flickering his one eyelid to Claude Mendibil, who translated his letters into words, into sentences, into paragraphs, into chapters and then to the completion of his book. This book was his Soulful Creation, a true masterpiece, sharing with the world the story of his life before and after his stroke. Jean-Dominique Bauby died 10 days after the publication of his creation, and before he died, he got to hear just how successful his book was.

12 Steps to Loving You is my first book, one of many I hope, and sitting down to write from my soul to yours took some time. How much more so for a man who did this by flickering his one eyelid? His passion was to rewrite The Count of Monte Cristo, but as a modern day version with a female, but the plot would still have been vengeance. He did not get to do this, but he did get to do something far greater. He got to share himself with the world, and now because of his book, we get to understand his journey, and hopefully others, with more depth, a greater awareness and a deep sense of compassion.

He did not 'disappear' when he had locked-in syndrome. He was just not able to communicate in the conventional way of speaking and writing. Jean-Do opens our eyes to the fact that where there is life, there is hope. Where there is breath, there is courage and where there is a will, there is creation.

Thank you Jean-Do for being the person who highlighted not just locked-in syndrome to me, but also allowed me to draw the parallels between being locked-in your body and being locked-in your mind through fear.

My eyes are still warm with tears when I think of Jean-Do. I wish I could reach out and stroke his cheek and tell him just how much his story has helped me over the years.

When we experience ourselves being locked-in our minds, through the vicious cycle of fear, then we will know what it is to be a prisoner of one's own making. This in itself is our own creation.

So why not create something different for yourself? Something so magical and beautiful, that even you will marvel at your own creation?

Close your eyes and focus on your gentle and deep breathing. That soulful blissful breathing that signals it is time to go on an inward journey. What you will find will amaze you. What you will find is the very core of who you are. No self-pity about the could-have-beens. No guilt about what has been and no fear about what is to be.

The time is now to focus on what you want to create. You have been given a large blank canvas with an easel, oil paints and paint brushes. You create a harmonious and light space to paint in, and you place your easel in the middle of your room.

You get to choose the colours you are going to use and the picture you are going to paint.

This culmination of painting will be your very own masterpiece, just as you would have it. You don't allow anyone else to come along and tell you what to paint, when to paint, what colours to use or what pictures would be best on your canvas. So why do you allow people to come into your life and tell you what they think is best for you, regardless of their intentions? Only you know what you truly want.

Far too often we cave in to other people's expectations, either through fear of standing up for ourselves or through some form of guilty obligation. When you are dependent on another, it creates all forms of difficulties and you need to ensure that you still own your own freedom of choice.

Choose wisely who you share your creation with. Some will criticise the strokes you make, the colours you choose and the progress of your painting. Some want the painting to be completed as soon as possible, and lack the finer art of patience.

Think for a moment just what it is you want to create when it comes to your family, friends, relationships, career, home and spiritual journey.

What is it that you hold dear in life? What is important to you? Your creations are unique – they have your unique mark all over it.

Don't let someone else take that away from you.

Now is the time to get proactive. Get your journal out and on the top of each page put the following headings:
1. Relationships
    a. What is your current relationship status?
    b. What status do you desire?
    c. What does your ideal partner look like?
    d. What is your ideal relationship?
2. Career
    a. Do you have a job?
    b. Do you love your current job?
    c. Do you want a job?
    d. Do you want a new job?
    e. What career aspirations do you have?
    f. What type of boss do you want?
    g. What working hours do you wish to work?
    h. Where do you wish to work?
3. Finances
    a. What is your current financial state of affairs?
    b. Are you in debt, and if so, how do you plan on getting out of debt?
    c. How much do you wish to earn?
    d. Are you saving your retirement?
    e. How much money do you want in your bank account?
    f. Do you own property?

g. Do you want to own property?

4. Family
    a. Are you starting a family of your own?
    b. What goals do you want to set for your family?
    c. Do you do things together?
    d. Are you a closely knit family?
    e. Do you have healthy family relationships?

5. Friends
    a. Have any of your existing friendships become toxic?
    b. Do you see your friends enough?
    c. Do you want to spend more time with your friends?
    d. What are your relationships like with your friends?
    e. What kind of relationship do you want with your friends?

6. Home
    a. What does your ideal home look like?
    b. What area do you want to stay in?
    c. What furniture and colours do you like?
    d. What are your neighbours like?
    e. Do you have a garden?

7. Self
    a. What clothes do you like to wear?

b. What colours suit you best?

c. What foods to you like to eat?

d. What is your ideal goal weight?

e. Can you see yourself having fun and laughing a lot?

f. Do you like taking vacations?

g. Do you like having time to read and unwind?

h. Do you take life too seriously?

i. Do you make enough time for yourself?

The above questions are to help you create a picture in your mind's eye as to what you want your life to look like. Whatever it is you choose will be picture perfect for you.

On each page, put your intentions for each category (and you can add more pages, e.g. for sport, health etc.). You can also get a pin board and put pictures of all the things you want to manifest into your life.

Put your vision board somewhere where you will see it daily. Breathe life into your creations by saying *thank you for …. that is in my life*. This might sound fake, but keep with it.

Believe that it is yours. Believe you are deserving of all that you have.

Let no-one tear down your dreams. They are yours. And once you have done all of this, breathe emotions of gratitude into your intentions that you have set.

Ask – Believe – Receive.

Cut pictures out of magazines and paste it in your journal. Adding pictures and emotions to the written word will help raise your vibrational energy to that of what you want in life.

The Universe will match this frequency, so if you live in a state of constant lack, then lack is what you will attract, but if you change this to creating an intention of wealth and abundance in your life, you need to show gratitude for what you already have and more of the same will be added.

Here are some more tips on how to create the life of your dreams:

1. Decide what you want out of life
2. Decide what you want to give back to life
3. Picture what you want with crystal clear clarity
4. Keep a journal of your intentions that you wish to manifest
5. Put your vision board in an area where you will see it daily
6. Start decluttering your space, i.e. your home, your car, your cupboards, your workspace and most importantly of all, your thoughts
7. Replace your negative thoughts of I can't to ones of I CAN!
8. Make space in your life for newness and positive change
9. Avoid the naysayers and your inner and outer critics

No matter where you are at in your life, things can change. You can change and your life can change. Change is not only for some, but for absolutely anyone at any stage in their lives.

You cannot get something new if you have a closed fist that is holding on tightly to the past. You have to loosen your grip on life and let your creation grow from your seed of intention.

Cheryl Richardson (life coach and author) said something so succinctly – *if you want milk, you don't go to the hardware store to get it*. So if you are looking for inspiration and support in your life, don't go to the naysayers or critics. Avoid those who bring you down and who try to manipulate you, regardless of their intentions. Rather, find likeminded individuals who will stand by and support you and who give you the freedom to be yourself without judgement or criticism.

A few people close to me have absolutely no idea of who I am, and this is due to no fault of their own. Either I have consciously not shared that part of my life with them, or they are closed minded and see life only as they believe it to be true. And the way they see life, is true to them. It does not have to be true for you. It can be difficult when you are in situations where you cannot avoid these people, but choose to be wise in what you do or do not share with them.

When it comes to your Soulful Creations, put all your heart and soul into it. Do not hold back, simply let go and just create. Your Soulful Creations will come to life when you infuse them with your emotions and desires. Your emotions are powerful magnets so use them wisely.

To get creative, open your mind and let go of the heaviness of your heart. Listen to some inspiring music, or take a walk in nature, watch an uplifting movie or spend time with people who make you feel good about yourself.

Once you feel that you are in your creative space, sit down to focus on what it is you want to have in this life.

Don't forget to have fun in the creation process. Do you want to write a book or start your own business? What creative adventures are you considering? One of the best ways to embark upon a creative adventure is to spend time with someone you consider to be your creative genius. Find out there methods of working. How do they plan their day? How did they get started? You will find that everyone had to start somewhere.

If creating your own destiny is foreign to you, then think of it as preparing for your road trip and then actually taking that road trip. For this road trip you need to pack the car and most importantly know where the end destination is. Once you know the end destination, you can plan the pit stops along the way.

The fun is in the journey, and not the destination – you will get there soon enough, but if you forget to have fun along the way (like I did for far too many years), then the journey will be tedious, dull and boring.

When I take long road trips, I ensure I have awesome music to drive with and a couple of audio books.

I sing along at the top of my lungs for the world to hear, and I enjoy every moment of the journey.

I am wary of who I take on long road trips with me, because they often want to go to other places which are not enroute to my destination.

So choose your travel companions wisely because you will be making compromises along the way. It is best to have a fellow traveler who wants to share the same or similar experiences with you. It just makes the journey that much more pleasurable.

Your life's journey is your ultimate Soulful Creation. You are creating your most Soulful Memories as you travel through this space and time. Make each moment count. Make each moment memorable. Make each moment truly your *joie de vivre* (a cheerful enjoyment of life).

What is the song that is within you? What song do you want to sing out to the world? Embrace this song and start singing. You are a beautiful human being doing the best you can – now go and create the dream life you have always wanted. It is never too late.

YOUR SOULFUL CREATIONS

1. Are you excited about creating the life of your dreams?

12 STEPS TO LOVING YOU

2. What does the life of your dreams look like, feel like, sound like?

3. Have you written your intentions in your journal? If not, don't delay and do it today – you need to do the work to allow manifestation to flow into your life.

4. What does your vision board look like?

5. What can you get rid of that will create space for the new to come in?

6. What intentions have you set for:

    a) Your family

    b) Your friendships

c)   Your career

d)   Your health

e)   Your finances

f)   Your home

g)   Your Self

h)   Your spiritual practice

AFFIRMATION FOR CHAPTER 8

I lovingly release all fear of my future and allow myself to create the life of my dreams without fear.

PHASE III

ALL ABOUT CREATION

CHAPTER 9
NATURE'S PATTERNS

I bathe in the river of righteousness
I soak in the sea of Self
I lie in the lake of Love
I wash away the worries of the world.
(Jennifer L. Breakey)

Nature is one of our most wonderful of teachers; if only we had eyes to see and ears to hear. Nature can teach us all there is to know about the flow of life. If only we would spend more time in nature, learning more than just about the birds and the bees.

Nature does not rush to get anything done. It simply just is.

When you plant a seed, you don't rush outside every day to see if shoots are pushing through the soil. You don't plant the seed and walk away, expecting it to grow without love and care. No, you water it, you provide it with nutrients through the compost you put in the soil. Neither do you give it too much or too little water. You get the balance just right, and provide whatever the seed needs to grow.

Not only does the seed require water and nutrients, but it requires light. Without light, nothing grows.

So it is with you. Think of a seed like your thought.

You have a thought – a positive one – and you will it to grow. So you tend to it often, by repeating the thought over and over again. Call this your affirmation. You think the thought and then you add layer upon layer of emotions on top of it.

With repetition comes belief and growth. The water and nutrients are the repetition that you give this thought. But without shining the light that you are on this thought, nothing will happen, because without light, life is not possible.

You tend to the seed, and it starts to grow. And a shoot sprouts from the ground. Elation and excitement fills your heart. Once the shoot appears, you don't walk away and leave it to come into full bloom. You don't expect it to fend for itself at such an early stage. No, you continue to provide it with love and light.

This is so often where people battle to continue the growth process and they give up far too easily. They allow all forms of distractions to divert their attention. This is just another trick of the ego.

They see a bit of life and are satisfied with this tiny bit of growth. Imagine if none of us ever gave up on something, but continued until it had grown full cycle? What an amazing world of accomplishments and completions we would create. So many people battle with completing projects, instead, jumping from one to another, without ever realising one creation in its entirety. Remember, a thought is just a thought until you add a bit of emotion and tender loving care to it.

Now that you have learnt to look after the seeds you plant, you find yourself with a garden.

Your garden is beautiful and multi-coloured with fragrances of all kinds. It attracts a variety of different kinds of birds, butterflies and bees. What a pleasure it is for you to sit in your garden, appreciating the joy and peace it brings.

Before long, you find yourself pre-occupied with life and all its trappings. Again, another trick of the ego.

Your life seems more and more out of sync, and you cannot fathom why this is happening. You notice you have not been showing up authentically. You decide to do an inventory of your thoughts, and what you find is disturbing.

You have left your garden unattended, and weeds (negative thoughts and grievances) have spread all over the place. You now have the daunting task of going within and pulling out the weeds. If you have ever gardened, you will know that weeding is only effective if you pull the weeds out, roots and all. And you will also know that some weeds are easier than others to pull out.

This is why meditation | quiet contemplation is so important for your well-being. This practice allows you to check in on yourself and by doing this you remove the weeds before they take root.

You learn to nip the negative thoughts in the bud, placing no emotion behind them, but rather you see them as clouds drifting on by.

When gardening, you need to know about the 4 cycles of the seasons – spring, summer, autumn, and winter – a never ending cycle.

This is like the cycle of life – birth, growth, maturity, death. None of us can escape this reality. It is what it is. The key is to learn how to live fully and joyfully in each cycle of life.

Each season dictates your actions. When you should be planting seeds and when you should be harvesting your crop. It also tells you when to clear the fields to make ready for the new harvest.

The four seasons can be our enemy or ally. It is all a matter of perception. Some people prefer summer to winter, whilst someone like me prefers the winter to summer. It is all a matter of personal taste.

The secret is not to hide from the seasons you do not like, but to embrace them all – wholeheartedly.

Spring is that beautiful time of the year when all things new are given the chance to be nurtured to grow. Birds are aplenty and butterflies fly lazily on by. New buds start opening and the breeze is cool on the skin.

The ice starts to melt and water starts flowing once again. Hibernating animals stretch and awaken to the blissful sounds of nature and the sights and warmth of the sun. It is a wondrous time of existence. It is a carefree time and a time for all things new.

As with all things, spring makes way for the summer, promising to return. Nothing is permanent – all things are temporal, and cyclical.

The sun's rays beats relentlessly on earth. The fullness of the fields is evident by the chirping of the crickets at night and the glorious colours of the summer sunsets. Love is all around. People seem happier, lighter. The once forgotten beaches, rivers and lakes, are again a haven for all types of creatures and water lovers. They swim for hours, enjoying the freedom that summer brings.

But summer cannot last forever, and it too has to make way for autumn. The leaves start to fall from the trees, birds start to migrate to warmer climates and people start to retreat into the comforts of the indoors. Trees are cut down to provide wood for the winter fires, as the logs crackle over the next few months. It can be quite an isolating time. People seem to be more distant, almost as if they have retreated within themselves. The laughter is not as noticeable when you go outdoors.

And then autumn takes its bow and heralds in the winter of our lives. Winter is a wondrous time, where warmth and companionship can be found by the fireside. It is a time to regroup together and spend some wonderful hours with loved ones. Some people are not so lucky.

This too can be the loneliest time of the year for those who have no family or friends.

The isolation is real, it is palpable and it is a reminder that the cycles of life all must come to an end, before they can begin again. So what happens in the spring, summer, autumn and winters of our lives. Let's take a look at each one separately.

In spring, you prepare for new possibilities that can be the birthing of something wonderful in your life. You nurture these possibilities and marvel at the wonders of everything around you. You prepare the land within for the newness that you are going to welcome into your reality. It is a joyous and creative time. You plant the seeds of your tomorrow, and you watch your shoots slowly begin to push themselves through the soil of your life.

Summer heralds the awakening of your wondrous creations. All your efforts start to pay off, and you see the fruits of your energetic inputs. You welcome the changes with open arms as you dance under the sun, moon and starlit sky. Love permeates your very being. Love for yourself, for others, for all living creatures, and for the earth and universe. Your senses are aroused to the wonders of your full life and it is here that your wonderful works are displayed for all to see. It is here that you consider the ways of your tomorrow. It is here that you can sit and enjoy the fruits of your labour.

As autumn slowly overshadows the summer sun, the leaves falling to the ground, you see that your creations have come to fruition and it is time to prepare for the winter days.

12 STEPS TO LOVING YOU

Your youthfulness is slowly ebbing out with the tide, and a new maturity takes over.

The youth start looking to you for guidance and wisdom, and you welcome this new phase of your life with an open heart and mind. You know that you are no longer the person you once were, and so you train the youth to run like champions, as you share your words of wisdom with them. You silently retreat into the knowledge of who you are and you are no longer consumed by the things that so heavily weighed on your heart. You shed your worries just like a tree sheds it leaves in the fall.

Winter has arrived. It is a cold season, a time for endings so that a way can be made for new beginnings. We bury our loved ones, knowing that we will be together again. Our lives change and this is a good thing. The sun is hidden and we are forced to take comfort from the fire and warm woolly blankets. Winter can be treacherous for many who do not have adequate provisions to take care of themselves. The homeless and stray animals are without warmth and have no certainty of survival. The winter of your life heralds in all things coming to an end. This is not a bad thing. It is just change. And an old adage reminds us that this too must come to an end: *sunshine comes after rain*.

Pay close attention to those going through the winter of their lives as you might just be the comfort they need during this season of change.

Let's consider the tempestuous ocean.

The tide ebbs and flows, just like things flowing in and out of our lives, being pulled by the power of the moon.

The sea can be calm and it can be dark, stormy and tumultuous. The sea can provide a safe passage of travel or it can swallow you up, only to spew you out along the shores of time. Either way, the ocean is to be respected. You cannot tame or control it. Your life too is calm and stormy, and you need to be able to adapt to this duality. The ocean is deep and dark and is often seen as symbolic of our spiritual connections to life. Pay close attention if you dream of the deep ocean, it is something deep within you that is sending you a message. Listen to nature's call.

Nature is truly a wonder, a marvel of never-ending imaginings. Our tempers can explode, which reminds us of the fiery volcano. A volcano erupts when the heat can no longer be contained due to the pressure beneath the earth's surface. Lava spills out, leaving destruction in its wake. So it is with your emotions. If you allow your emotions to erupt in violence, anger or hate, it will spill over and also leave destruction wherever it flows. Its damage is devastating, oftentimes hurting those who are innocent bystanders.

Anger is but one letter away from danger. When you feel an eruption about to take place, take a step back and just breathe. Breathe slow deep breaths, which will trick your brain into thinking that all is calm, helping you to avoid unnecessary hurt and devastation.

So many people have the innate ability to bottle things up inside, until that one word or deed sends them in a spiral of outbursts.

This leaves the bystander at a loss for words, not knowing quite what has happened. For the giver of the outburst, it is like the straw that broke the camel's back. They could no longer contain their anger and they just blurt it out in one episode. This is incredibly destructive and an unhealthy way to treat your body. Storing all that anger in your body is not only toxic, but it is also emotionally debilitating. It is important to learn to communicate healthily when things are bothering you, right at the outset. Don't be the person who lives with regret, because once you have done or said something, you cannot take it back. It is etched in the carvings of life.

Rain is a blessing from the heavens. Our survival depends on water, the elixir of life. Some people know how to dance in the rain, whilst others remain indoors, all huddled up and trying to keep warm. When the clouds get too heavy with condensation, the rain falls to the ground. This is the same with our tears. When our soul gets too heavy with sadness, the tears fall down our cheeks. Both the rain and tears are cleansing. Tears are a way of releasing sadness, and yet they can also be tears of joy.

Thus tears are a by-product of a very strong emotion. It allows these emotions to flow from our bodies. Don't hold back the tears. If you need to cry, then cry.

The saying that big boys don't cry is actually quite damaging. Big boys do and should cry. Perhaps if big boys cried, the world would not be in such a mess that it currently finds itself in.

Nature can teach us so much if we would just listen and watch.

Be kind to yourself and go out into nature and see what lessons you can learn. Then go and share those lessons with others.

We encroach on nature's frontlines, threatening to bring the human species to its knees. Think before it is too late. Respect and preserve the earth, as it provides vitality for you and for generations to come. When all the land is exploited, there will be nothing left to sustain our planet and then it will be too late to turn back the hand of time.

Not only are we destroying nature and whole ecosystems, but we are also destroying the habitat of fellow travellers. How would you feel if someone came to your hometown and started pillaging everything in sight? Everything you love and hold dear, being torn down, leaving ruin in its wake. Not a pleasant thought compared to the thought of all of humanity living in harmony.

This is achievable. Let's strive for a harmonious existence with all. Let's love ourselves enough to want the best for everyone, for what you do to one, you do to yourself. Let's follow the example of nature and find a balance of mutual co-habitation.

Stop – Think – Listen – Apply.

YOU AND NATURE'S PATTERNS

1. What cycle of life are you in – spring, summer, autumn or winter?

2. What cycle of life are your family members in? It is important to know this, as each season has different attributes, and you should be aware of this.

3. What do you enjoy most about the current cycle of life that you are in?

4. What does the garden of your life look like? Is it orderly or haphazard? None is right or wrong, it is all about personal taste.

5. When last have you done an inventory of your life's garden?

6. Go into your garden and look for weeds – do you find any? If you did, then begin the clean-up process. Then make this a daily habit.

7. What parallels can you draw between nature and your own life?

8. If you could paint the garden of your life, what would you paint? What colours would you use?

9. How often do you spend time in nature? Are you able to go out into nature more, and if so, when will you start?

AFFIRMATION FOR CHAPTER 9

I am one with nature and I allow myself to see all the lessons that nature has to show me. I respect earth and all its inhabitants.

CHAPTER 10
WONDER-FILLED MEANDERINGS

The river winds its way lazily to the ocean,
seeing sights and sounds of energy in motion.
There is no rush, no need for speed,
just an ever winding journey
of lightness on the breeze.
(Jennifer L. Breakey)

If you slow down and quieten your mind, you will hear the rhythmic sound of your heart beating. What a miracle this is; the beating of your heart, giving you life so that you can fully enjoy this human experience. Blood flows through your veins, pumping through the central station of your heart.

The wonder-filled meandering of life is gentle, it is slow and it is an opportunity for you to take in all the wonderful sights and sounds along your life's journey.

How often do you hear the sound of your heart beating? If you are anything like so many other people, your life's pace is far too rushed and frenetic to take time out to stop and just listen to your heart beat.

Sometimes the first time you become aware of your heartbeat, is when you experience heart palpations, from built up stress and anxiety.

Try this as an exercise to see how much you rely on technology. Go off the grid for a weekend – no newspapers, no TV, no phones, no laptops, no outside communication with the world. This is considered a luxury and sometimes this is not a priority in your life. Why is that?

I love a quote from the Tao Te Ching – *I do nothing and nothing is left undone.* It speaks of no striving, just peaceful gliding through this space in time and yet everything still gets done.

What if the way we live our lives is nothing short of a distraction from what we are here to experience? What if we are here to learn to *listen, see, feel and experience this gift of life*? The paradox is that life throws distractions at us so that we spend our lives calving out some existence that will help look after us in our twilight years? And that is based on the presupposition that we will in fact make it to our twilight years.

Cancer and stress are two top known killers in our society and we are bombarded of these statistics daily. This exasperates the premise that we might just be the unwilling recipient of one, if not both, of these daunting statistics. Today you read that the new number one killer is supposed to be boredom. I am bowled over by this statistic.

Do we live our lives in accordance with the amount of stimulation we can put into it? Do we need to jam-pack our lives with busyness and have we really strayed so far from the truth that we have forgotten who we are? Have we forgotten how to appreciate the ever changing scenery in our lives? Have we forgotten how to be still and to just go with the flow?

We spend our lives in search of a quest, the Holy Grail, only to come full circle and realise we have forgotten what the quest and Holy Grail was all about.

We have become satisfied with our life just as it is, experiencing this to be the norm. We have misplaced this quest, searching instead for achievement, accumulation, success, and the glittering gold of life but we cannot see that the magic and the miracle of life is in fact us. Our human existence is a symbiosis with the universe. And if this is in fact true, then why are we not embodying the laws of the universe, learning how to be a creator in our lives, a co-creator with the Source of all. And who is this Source of all that is? It is God, the intelligent mind, the Creator of all, the pure Love that has always been, always is and always will be. We cannot even begin to fathom the truth of God. God is our awakened consciousness.

In the early hours of this morning, around about 3am, I got up and lay on the couch in my lounge, snug under a warm blanket, just thinking about God. I remembered a question I once posed to Neale Donald Walsh. I asked him *why we call God – God*.

After having read the Tao Te Ching, it made sense to me that by the mere fact that we call the Tao – the Tao, we limit the Tao by this very act. And I have always felt this about calling God – God. I never wanted to fall into a trap of limiting God in my life, by the fact that I have placed the Source of all into a box of my own limited human understanding.

For example, if I said to you dog, what comes to mind? You will invariably think of a four-legged animal, man's best friend. Or do you think of a ferocious animal that you fear intensely? Your reaction is based solely on your own personal experiences and knowledge of what a dog is.

The same applies to God. If I say God, then immediately we conjure up an image in our mind of what we have either been taught through our religious and spiritual experiences. But this is a futile attempt of trying to understand the unfathomable. It is preposterous and an injustice served on the reality of who God truly is. God cannot be defined. Not in one secular form of teaching.

I felt a sense of frustration rising. Why does God not appear to me in human form and sit and have coffee with me? This would make my life so much easier and we could talk about all sorts of matters of the heart. How can I break out of the silence I have built around me, so that my voice can reach far and wide, opening people up to the truth of the Source.

When people ask me who I would like to have tea with, any person either dead or alive, my answer remains the same, Jesus Christ and Albert Einstein.

For now, I am not able to sit down in the physical with either Jesus Christ or Albert Einstein, but I believe that when you cross over to the other realm, you are in your new form of pure spirit, pure Love.

You are not bound by time and space, so this reality deduces that you can still commune with them, regardless if they have already crossed over to the other realm. If you want to read a book that will give you so much clarity, insight, hope and inspiration about the life hereafter, then I highly recommend you read Anita Moorjani's book – Dying to be Me.

I visited Albert Einstein's home in Bern, Switzerland, and stood by the desk where he once worked. I was hoping to sense something about the man behind the theories.

Maybe I would pick up on his intelligent mojo – I guess that is what you could call wishful thinking, but it was a wonderful experience.

I walked the footpaths that he would have walked, visited the parks he would have frequented, and our confines to time and space was very real to me.

After lying on the couch for a while, I went back to the warm comfort of my own bed.

I knew deep within me that although I could not physically commune with God over a cup of coffee, I could be still and notice how God is within each of us, and that I need to still myself long enough to truly hear from this Oneness.

I believe in the quantum pool of knowledge, where we have all the inner guidance that we need, we just need to be willing and receptive to tap into this resource. All you need to do is say – *I am willing to open my heart and mind to the Universe and I allow my inner guidance to lead me. I am willing to step aside from human intellect and to allow Source to pervade every cell of my being. I am willing to move from my head to my heart.*

We all have a point where we enter the river of life here on earth. We are destined to meander our way down to the ocean of Love, our final resting place, where we all meet together in unison, as one expansive pool of pure Love. It is how we travel down this river that will determine the experiences we have in this lifetime. Sometimes the river flows gently towards the expansive ocean. Other times, the river forms eddies and we become stuck and stagnant, going around and around in the same place without any seeming way out of this never ending cycle of perpetual circular motion. And sometimes there are rapids and waterfalls along the way.

You need to be an experienced river navigator, managing the rhythm of the flowing water.

The subtle changes in the speed of the river are barely noticeable at first, but when the speed picks up, you become more aware of its changes in your conscious reality.

If you would notice the joys in not trying to swim against the currents, but to rather trust, let go and go with the flow, you will see that the journey of life can be easy and effortless, if only you would allow yourself to merge as one with the river of your life.

As you go along your wonder-filled meanderings, you will notice different sceneries along the way. You will notice the weeping willows, the outstretched endless rolling hills, the built up areas, the pollution in some parts of the river, and the clear blue skies above. You would learn to acknowledge your fellow travelers, helping them out if you see they have got stuck in an eddy along the way.

You are not travelling these unchartered waters alone. Many have gone before you and many will come after you. And many are with you now.

You are not undertaking this journey on your own. We are all in this together. We appear separate, but this is a lie, because we are all connected to one another. Lie back in your canoe, take out your picnic basket, and begin to enjoy the views and greet those you meet along the way.

The river will reach the ocean soon enough, and then it will be time for you to merge with the pool of pure Love. You will have arrived at your destination, you will have arrived home.

Lao Tzu asks us all to live by the 4 virtues of life:
1. Reverence for all – respect
2. Sincerity – honesty
3. Gentleness – kindness
4. Supportiveness – being of service

If, along your journey, you can ask how can I be reverend, how can I show kindness, how can I be honest and how can I be of service, you will be doing all that you need to know along your wonder-filled meandering of life.

We all want to profoundly touch the lives of others, and by living these virtues, you can do just this. Remember, *you are only a thought away from living your best life* – Dr. Wayne W. Dyer.

So imagine yourself in your canoe, pushing off from the edge and heading towards your destination. Don't worry, the currents will take you. You are not alone and you are a more capable navigator than you give yourself credit for.

You have your inner built-in compass; let your internal GPS guide you. Let go of holding on so tightly to the river banks and let yourself drift out into the middle of the river, then ease that angst you feel within yourself, and let the flow of life direct you in all your ways.

You have got this. You can do this. You are not alone. Not now or ever. You have never been alone and you will never be alone.

Start opening up to the captain of your journey and be guided by your intuition and higher Self.

Do you remember that song – *so long ago, too far apart, couldn't wait another day for the Captain of my Heart*? (Victor Lazlo)

Well here is the good news; the Captain has always been ready and waiting. Waiting for you to settle in, let go of the ropes which secure you to the land. Let go and start drifting in the wondrous gift of life.

YOUR WONDER-FILLED MEANDERINGS

1. What kind of navigator are you – nervous or comfortable? Do you trust your own intuition or do you rely on others to show you the way?

2. Are you aware of the sceneries of your life, or are you letting everything just rush on by?

3. Are you a person who likes to be in tight control or are you relaxed and easy going?

4. Close your eyes and take a look around you now. Notice the scenery on the riverbanks. What do you see? Where are you at in your life?

5. Has your canoe become stuck in an eddy? If so, see yourself gently taking your oars and rowing out of the eddy.

6. Are you rowing against or with the current of life?

7. What ways can you relax and enjoy the flow of life?

8. What is holding you back from being adventurous and exploring new meanderings?

9. How easy is it for you to take control of rowing your own canoe?

10. Is there anything in your canoe that is weighing you down and making the rowing that much more difficult? If so, let it go. It no longer serves you and you will be lighter and freer than ever before?

AFFIRMATION FOR CHAPTER 10

I am willing to open my heart and mind to the Universe and I allow my inner guidance to lead me. I am willing to step aside from human intellect and allow God to pervade every cell of my being. I am willing to move from my head to my heart.

CHAPTER 11
CONSCIOUS LIVING

If you love yourself you love others.
If you hate yourself you hate others.
In relationships with others, it is only you, mirrored.
(Osho)

To live a fully conscious life you need to acknowledge that you have an ego whose sole purpose is to hide your true identity. Your ego shouts so loud that it drowns out that still small voice within you. It places a veil between your authentic self and your false identity.

Your ego says that you are your accomplishments, your social status, your financial status, your materialistic things and qualifications that you have acquired. It denies that you are a Spark of the Divine.

You need to practice dropping the ego when it raises its head and practice going within, as covered in the first 10 chapters of this book, to uncover your true identity.

The first 10 chapters of this book have taken you on an inward journey of self-discovery.

There is no place for fear, guilt, regrets or self-loathing.

We all make mistakes; some big and some small; but it is in the letting go of these all too familiar attachments that we give ourselves the much needed space to finally come home to our true selves, just as we are.

A Course in Miracles defines sin as *a lack of love*. It was an error in judgement and any error can be rectified. You don't need to berate yourself over and over for things you could have done differently. Let go of your judgement. That is true change.

The first 10 steps take you on an inner quest, a search for who you are:

Step 1 – energy – all that is

Step 2 – who are you?

Step 3 – authenticity

Step 4 – change your thinking to change your life

Step 5 – healing the hurt

Step 6 – grounding tools for your journey

Step 7 – soulful integrations

Step 8 – soulful creations

Step 9 – nature's patterns

Step 10 – wonder-filled meanderings

It is important that before you begin the next two and final chapters of this book that you do the exercises truthfully and honestly in each of the above chapters, because it is here that you will learn to apply all that you have brought to the light.

It is here that you will realise the true magnificence of who you are and you will learn that you are more lovable than you could ever have imagined, and more deserving than you realise. *You are a bright shining star, a radiant beam of light. You are Love personified. You are a wondrous creation of the Universe and you have every right to be here. Don't let anyone dull your shine. Don't be afraid to let your light shine brightly for all to see. Find your voice and rejoice in being heard.*

Something I am often faced with is how do you do a 360 turnabout change when your family and friends have come to expect you to be a certain way? My answer is simple. Change is inevitable. We all know it is the only constant in life. And with change, you will leave some relationships behind, not out of judgement, but because the relationships have played out their course in your life and they no longer serve your good.

My life has been a rollercoaster ride of change. I denied my true passions and calling because I feared failure and being ridiculed by my peers. I was a people pleaser, like so many, and I did not want to disappoint anybody.

I could not see how to bring my passion to life, as it is not the acceptable norm and not what others would expect of me.

This fear propelled me forward and I lost a lot of money and energy in the process.

I also unwillingly hurt some really nice people along the way for which I have had to forgive myself, and through this letting go, I have had to learn to ignore other people's opinions of me. Instead, I send them love and blessings when they judge or persecute me, even though they are family and are coming from the space of their own unconsciousness and hurt.

You are not someone's opinion of you. You are who you are – you are pure love and delight and you are doing the best you can with the resources you have. Don't attack yourself, choose to love yourself instead. This is empowering.

To know how to live a conscious life, it is best for you to look at what an unconscious daily existence looks like. In this way, you will be able to determine your own level of consciousness.

1. The alarm clock goes off at 5am. You wearily reach over and press the snooze button. Just 5 more minutes is all you need before you stumble out of bed and roll into the office.
2. Bleary eyed, you get out of bed and go straight to the kettle. You put the kettle on, fill the cup with your morning caffeine injection and then find yourself washing your hair in the shower.
3. In the background you hear the news that spools all the depressing happenings in the world around you. You unconsciously absorb the information, put on your work clothes, promise yourself a muffin at the corner store and head out the door.

12 STEPS TO LOVING YOU

4. You get in your car and head out into the morning traffic. Bumper to bumper, you slowly move forward, to a job which has long lost its lustre and excitement for you. It is now just a means to pay all the bills.
5. Your day is one of telephone calls, complaining customers, angry bosses, disgruntled employees and whining subordinates. By the time you look at the clock, it is home time, and you notice for the first time that day that you have not had your lunch break yet.
6. Again you head on out and climb into your car. You find yourself back in the bumper to bumper evening traffic and slowly you head on home for a TV dinner and some mindless series that you watch so that you can fill the void of silence.

This is a normal day for you and your weekends consist of seeing a few friends, watching some sport, having a few drinks and trying to catch up on much needed sleep. This is all about to change.

As you begin to awaken to all the wondrous possibilities that life could be, you start to see a glimmer of hope on the horizon.

You see the sun gently peeking from behind the clouds of discontent and you are willing to take a chance on a new way of being.

You are prepared to ask yourself what if there is another way.

What if you can change your life by changing your thoughts? What if this is not all there is to life and that perhaps you made a wrong turn a while back, but you can now take a detour and head in the direction of your dreams.

And you begin to see this as an adventurous game, with nothing to lose, and everything to gain.

But how do you bring consciousness into your daily activities? How do you begin to awaken in a world where you have been asleep for so long?

The answer will amaze you as it is simple, easy, effortless and effective. No extra energy is required when it comes to changing your thoughts. You do this through grace and thinking differently. All you have to do is to begin the process by being willing to see things differently.

We are able to rewire the programming in our brains, so that they light up differently. Through creating new dendrites (neurological pathways), you will create new habits and new thoughts, just by the mere repetition of affirmations. We briefly discussed dendrites in Chapter 3, and it is something that can help you understand how you can change your way of thinking.

1. Dendrites is from the Greek word déndron, 'tree', and they are branched projections of a neuron that act to transmit the electrochemical stimulation received from other neural cells to the cell body, or soma, of the neuron from which the dendrites project.

2. Dendritic branching helps make connections between cells.
3. As cells connect with other cells, synapses occur – a synapse is a junction between two nerve cells, consisting of a minute gap across which impulses pass by diffusion of a neurotransmitter.
4. New synapses appear after learning.
5. Repeating earlier learnings make neural pathways more efficient through myelination (fatty substance formed around axons).

You can change your thinking by applying the following:

1. Watch your thoughts *like a hawk*, not just for one day, but for a whole month. Really watch your thoughts. Commit to doing the work, and the results will change your life forever. Isn't this wonderful?
2. Become aware of your thought patterns without judgement.
3. When you notice a negative thought, just watch it float in and out of your view (remember, you are the deep blue sky and your thoughts are the clouds floating on by). Attach no emotion to this, as emotions add fuel to the thought.
4. For every negative thought you have, replace it by repeating the exact opposite (for example, if you catch yourself saying 'no-one loves me', replace this with 'I am a child of the Universe and I am loved for all eternity – I am lovable and I am worthy', and repeat this at least 5 to 10

times each time you catch yourself having the same negative thought).

5. Set positive affirmations and place these on post-its around the house and in your car. These are constant reminders which will help you create new thinking patterns.

6. Dendrites are neurological pathways and new ones can be created and old ones can be destroyed.

7. You create new dendrites through learning and repetition. And learning is a step by step process. So start at the very beginning and build on from that.

8. You will see that when you stop your negative thoughts in their tracks, they will eventually become less and less until they are no longer a part of your thinking patterns.

9. The same goes for when you repeat positive affirmations – when you say them enough times (it was first thought to be 21 times, and now there is new research that says it is 66 times –let's just say it is quite a few times – you will find what works for you), they will start to become an automatic way of thinking, and this is what you want.

10. Your thoughts are just mirroring your belief system to you, and by watching your thoughts, you will start to healthily question your belief system. It is never too late to adjust what you believe.

11. When working on your belief system, ask yourself the following:

12 STEPS TO LOVING YOU

   a.   Where did this belief come from?
   b.   How long have I had this belief?
   c.   Is it possible that this belief no longer holds true for me?
   d.   Is this belief based on love or fear?
   e.   Does this belief serve my higher good?
12. Changing your thoughts requires active participation on your part.
13. Once you start changing your thoughts for the better, your life will start to change for the better too.
14. Change your thinking to change your life is now the reality you need to start living a conscious life.

Once you have mastered your thoughts, all else will start to fall into place. This is an ongoing process. It is always most difficult to begin this process, but it does become a way of being, and will help you live the life you have always dreamed of living.

YOUR CONSCIOUS LIVING CHECKPOINTS

1. Describe your normal week day?

2. Did you have to think about what your normal week day looks like? If so, this means that you operate on auto-pilot and you need to be more conscious throughout your day.

3. How much coffee do you drink per day? Do you take sugar with your coffee? Coffee and sugar are like shots of energy flowing through your veins. This gives you a sudden high and then an even quicker low. Try to lessen your coffee and sugar intake and see how this makes you feel. You might feel awful to begin with, but after a while you will start to see a positive difference.

4. How much TV do you watch in a week? How much of this is negative viewing? What fun things can you replace watching TV with?

5. How aware are you of emotional shifts in your body?

6. What old habits do you want to let go of?

7. What new habits do you want to create?

AFFIRMATION FOR CHAPTER 11

I am a bright shining star, a radiant beam of light. I am Love personified. I am a wondrous creation of the Universe and have every right to be here.

CHAPTER 12
YOUR SACRED JOURNEY

Live a life that matters
Not only just for you
But live a life that matters
One of service to others too
(Jennifer L. Breakey)

Waking up each morning, I learnt from Dr. Wayne W. Dyer to say *thank you – thank you – thank you*. It helps to set my focus and intention for the day. Thank you for the life I have been given. Thank you for this wondrous gift called life. Thank you for another glorious day here on planet earth.

It is not always easy; in fact, sometimes life can be filled with seemingly endless strife. That is just a reminder of our humanity. If it were not for the troubles we face each day, how would we grow? Without fear, how would we understand that perfect Love casts out all fear? There is a place for everything. The lessons ebb and flow in our lives. If we experienced no hardship and difficult relationships, how would we know what forgiveness is?

We are called to love one another. To remind each other that we are not separate, but that we are all connected on our journey homeward.

We are here to bless, serve and help one another. We are here to be a shining light to the world.

How would you describe your life right now, in this very moment? Are you content with where you are at or can you see opportunities for change? Are you truly happy and at peace, or have you lost your *joie de vivre*? If you saw your life as a marble, how bright is its shine, or is it dull and lacklustre?

The beauty is that no matter where you are at in your life, it can change from today.

To love yourself is the foundation for a life well lived. To truly love yourself, regardless of any mistakes you have made, is the best gift that you will ever give yourself. You have chastised yourself for far too long. It is time to let your hard outer casing fall away. Let love melt the barriers that stand between who you think you are and who you really are. Let the veil be lifted and the scales fall off your eyes. Go within and say gently, *'thank you that the veil is lifted and that my heart is reawakening to all the wonders of the world and to the truth of who I am'*.

You are deserving just as you are; everything else is a lie. A lie to keep you from finding your true identity. You are a miraculous spiritual being having a human experience.

You will notice that as soon as you soften to yourself, you will become soft with others. Instead of being snappy and irritable, you will have compassion and understanding in its place.

You will have patience and tolerance and a deep ability to hold others in your heart. You will start traveling this journey with ease, grace, compassion, love and joy.

In his book *Aleph*, Paulo Coelho writes in the first person, as a man wrestling with his spiritual stagnation. In the language of technical mathematics, Aleph means the number that contains all numbers, but in this story it represents a mystical voyage wherein two people experience a spiritual unleashing that has a profound impact on their present lives.

What is the Aleph?

1. The first letter of the Hebrew Alphabet.

2. The numerical value of Aleph is 111 (Aleph + Lamed + Peh: 1 + 30 + 80 = 111).

3. The number 111 contains the trinity; and it is also the constant of the magic square of six.

4. 111 = 1 + 10 +100 – symbolically this means that the Aleph combines the Divine, the Spiritual and the Physical world.

Whether you are on a journey through Russia travelling the length of the Trans-Siberian railroad, as in the Aleph, or whether you are sitting in some remote location or amidst the hustle and bustle of everyday life, your life will always be a sacred journey.

Whether you are standing still or moving forward, this is all a part of your life's journey.

You are moving through linear time to get from point A to point B. Point A is when you were born and point B is when you arrive at your final destination, home, the life hereafter, where we all meet again.

Horizontal time is not real, everything happens simultaneously (the past, present and future), but we are unable to compute this, so we have created the past, present and future to be able to define our existence in relation to time. A Course in Miracles reminds us that time is temporal and will cease to be when it is no longer useful as a learning aid.

Your sacred journey is one to be enjoyed and lived to the fullest. The word *sacred* comes from the Latin 'sacer'. A person may be designated as sacred, and so can objects or a place which is regarded as *extraordinary or unique*. The word *'sacer'* is closely related to 'numen' meaning *mysterious power* or *God*. Numinous (spiritual, mystical, magic, magical) is used to describe the Sacred to indicate its power.

You are a Divine creation. You are more than your physical body and thoughts. Find your sacredness within and walk in the knowledge that you are more than just a reflection staring back at you in the mirror. God is within you, as you.

Therein lies your true Divinity. There are many truths, choose the one that resonates with you. You need to honour the Truth within you. This is your Sacred Journey.

You need never feel ashamed of the Truth within you. The Truth is yours. You do not need to explain it to anyone. You need to live your Truth, embrace it, share it when you feel called to do so, and cherish it all the days of your life.

Sometimes your journey will take you off on some truly interesting detour. Do not fear this change. Rather enjoy the new sights and sounds, and connect with others along the way. You do not need to visit all the sacred places or have an Eat Pray Love moment. You can experience a satori (instant awakening) wherever you are. The sacredness is within.

Let's look at the vehicle you are using for this journey. How do you look after your car? Do you fill it up with petrol or diesel, check the oil and water and tyres, every time you go to the gas station? Do you take your vehicle in for regular services and ensure that the spare tyre is in good condition?

Do you have the necessary tools in your car that you will need if you have a flat tyre? Do you have roadside assistance? There are so many other questions to ask regarding your vehicle, but these are the most important ones.

If you take good care of your car, you will not let it run on empty. You will check the water and oil levels and tyre pressure. Your spare will be in good condition and your tools will be secured in the boot of your car.

The same goes for your physical body. Your body is a vessel that carries you through life. You get to choose whether you abuse it or whether you treat it with the love and respect it is due. My weight has fluctuated over the years, and this has been noticeably linked to the stress I experienced at the time. Now that this is in my awareness, I can do something about it.

I do not smoke and rarely drink alcohol, but I know that there is so much more I could be doing to look after my body. It is well within my ability to control what I put in my mouth, and it is something I consciously need to work on. And this is okay. I am not hard on myself, and I need to ensure it is well fed, gets exercise and sufficient sleep.

Less stress and anxiety is urgently needed. We fill our bodies with all forms of anti-anxiety pills and other prescribed drugs.

Whilst there is a place for modern medicine, much of it can be eradicated by a change in lifestyle.

A more peaceful and compassionate way of living is necessary to ensure our survival.

But how do we attain this in our maddening society and in the fast pace life we have grown far too accustomed to?

How do we let go of what is and embrace what is yet to come? How do we have faith when so much devastation is evident? How do we forgive ourselves and others for the hurt inflicted upon us, humanity and earth? How do we truly forgive, and move forward in the way of the lightness of being?

We start by seeing the bigger picture. We start by seeing that we are all on a journey through this wondrous experience on earth. We start by seeing that there is more to why we are here than we once believed to be true.

And we start to believe that it is okay to love ourselves deeply. This is not narcissism. This is a real love story in the making. A love story so profoundly real, that it will shake the very foundation of all that we see and do. We are love. We are created in our Creator's image. We are spirit, of Spirit. We are all One, connected in this wondrous web of life.

To all those gone before us, thank you for paving the way for us. To all those on our journey with us, may we learn to be of service to you, and to all those to come, tread lightly on this earth.

Go compassionately in the wake of the Great Awakening. Let Spirit in. Let your Light shine forth.

Let the world see you for who you are - a truly magnificent and wonderful spiritual being having a human existence.

Go within and find the lessons that you are here to learn. Then learn them.

I am here to learn to dissolve the illusion of fear and guilt. I am here to learn to take control of my emotional states and to only let the pureness of Love and Joy in.

I am here to be of service to everyone who wants to learn to truly Love themselves, regardless of what their families and friends think of them and regardless of what they think of themselves.

I am here to be of service to the workplace – lighting the truth and revealing all that is hidden.

I am here to bring Love back to its rightful place in the workplace. And I am here to let you know that it is okay to:

1. love yourself with all your heart
2. be a workplace giant
3. be a conquering crusader

You are born for greatness and with Love in your heart. Let your song fill the air.

Let your life be a fragrant offering to the Source of All that Is and let your peace lead your onwards, for another day.

YOU AND YOUR SACRED JOURNEY

1. How has your sacred journey treated you so far?

2. What are the greatest lessons you have learnt up until now?

3. What lessons are you here to learn and how can you be of service to others?

AFFIRMATION FOR CHAPTER 12

My eyes are now open and the veil has been lifted. I see my Divinity – God lives in me as me. I am on a wondrous journey full of adventures, and there is more to why I am here than I once believed.

AFTERWORD

Congratulations on starting this process of self-love. This is the best gift you can give yourself. We all make mistakes and most of us are our own worst critics. We say things to ourselves that we would never dream of saying to our friends. Why is this? Why are we so hard on ourselves, when life is hard enough on its own? We need to embrace our Divinity. We are here to live a life of Joy and Love, without exception. We are here to remove all the barriers that stand between us and Love. And to help you do just that, you have successfully completed the following steps:

- Step 1 – energy – all that is
- Step 2 – who are you?
- Step 3 – authenticity
- Step 4 – change your thinking to change your life
- Step 5 – healing the hurt
- Step 6 – grounding tools for your journey
- Step 7 – soulful integrations
- Step 8 – soulful creations
- Step 9 – nature's patterns
- Step 10 – wonder-filled meanderings
- Step 11 - conscious living
- Step 12 – your sacred journey

Here are the affirmations for each chapter:

1. Everything I see and do not see is energy. I have full control over the energy in my body, surroundings and circumstances.
2. I am not my insecurities or fears. I am loved beyond measure.
3. My actions and words are congruent with my beliefs and values. I always show up authentically, and unashamedly so.
4. I change my habitual thought-patterns easily and effortlessly. I only think thoughts that are for my higher good.
5. I let go of all hurts and grievances and replace them with Love.
6. I have all the resources I need to live a fully actualised and balanced life.
7. I joyously integrate all aspects of my life.
8. I lovingly release all fear of my future and allow myself to create the life of my dreams.
9. I am one with nature and I allow myself to see all the lessons that nature has to show me. I respect earth and all its inhabitants.
10. I am willing to open my heart and mind to the Universe and I allow my inner guidance to lead me. I am willing to step

aside from human intellect and to allow God to pervade every cell of my being. I am willing to move from my head to my heart.

11. I am a bright shining star, a radiant beam of light. I am Love personified. I am a wondrous creation of the Universe and have every right to be here.

12. My eyes are now open and the veil has been lifted. I see my Divinity – God lives in me as me. I am on a wondrous journey full of adventures, and there is more to why I am here than I once believed.

Reading this book and doing the exercises is merely a starting point for you to truly see yourself as the masterpiece that you are. There is no one correct way to live your life – there is only the way that feels right for you. When you know what that way is, embrace it and live your truth wholeheartedly.

Do not shy away from who you are. Embrace who you are with love and acceptance. Set yourself free by doing the hard work of forgiving yourself for letting yourself down. Forgive others for hurting you.

Remove the outer casings of your heart and let your light shine for the entire world to see. Darkness is just the absence of light. Fear is just the absence of Love. So let Love and Light guide you in all you do.

This is an awakening process. You are not in competition with anyone else. Begin to enjoy your life because life is short and your time on earth will be over soon enough. So love those who are on this path with you, have a grateful heart for this experience, and let go of all the guilt and fear that weigh you down.

You are not alone. There are so many others going through the same experience. Be kind, compassionate and gentle with yourself and others, for each one of us has our own scars to prove we are having this human experience.

Let Love and Light be your Guide.

ACKNOWLEDGEMENTS

There are so many people I would like to thank, and I cannot mention them all. So to everyone who has been a part of my life and helped me awaken to who I truly am, I am eternally grateful. Blessings, Love and Peace to you all.

To the wise ones who have helped me along the way, I thank the late Dr. Wayne W. Dyer, the late Louise Hay, Anita Moorjani, Lisa Natoli, the late Albert Einstein and Gregg Braden, for giving me so much to contemplate, learn and apply in my life. You have each touched my soul in such a delightful way.

Thank you to John Sanei for giving me the courage to get my message out to the world – thank you for blazing the trail before me, thus leading by example.

I thank my dear friend Dr. Laura Kleinhans, for her patience with the fruition of this book and for your friendship over the years. You are truly a remarkable woman, and one I am glad is a part of my life.

To Jacqueline Jones, you are truly an angel on earth. Your kindness to everyone you meet is an example for us all. You sacrifice so much for so many and I truly am eternally grateful that I can call you friend. Thank you for believing in me, even when I had given up believing in myself.

To my family, thank you for all the lessons you have brought into my life and thanks to those of you who stood by me through the good and bad times.

To my daughter Julia Breakey, Jules – I love you like no other. From the moment you were conceived I loved you and I always will. Thank you for being so strong when I could not be. Thank you for being the best daughter a mother could ever ask for. Thank you for being the Love in my life. You are a true miracle and your mother's delight.

And lastly, thank you God for putting up with my rantings. For steadfastly showing me how much I am loved. Thank you for opening my eyes to the truth and softening my heart. Thank you for being my eternal Love and resting place. I love you without measure.

ABOUT THE AUTHOR

Jennifer L. Breakey grew up in Cape Town, South Africa, and lived for a few years in London and Switzerland. At the age of 3 years old to 10 years old, Jennifer lived at Nazareth House in Cape Town, where she learnt very valuable lessons in life. These lessons have helped her help countless people in learning how to forgive themselves and others, and learning how to let go of the past. It was here that Jennifer learnt to be resilient, optimistic and ever hopeful.

Jennifer has studied in a variety of disciplines, both academic and esoteric, and she worked in executive roles in Human Resources, in the workplace. Jennifer has a firm understanding of the employment relationship and is a keen advocate of rightful behaviour in the workplace.

Jennifer's love and passion is to extend Love and Healing to the world, to help businesses develop and grow Workplace Giants and to awaken the world to become Conscious Crusaders.

Jennifer is currently studying to be a Licensed Unity Teacher, and she is an avid student of A Course in Miracles. Jennifer currently lives in Cape Town, South Africa.

NOTES

NOTES

NOTES

NOTES

Printed in Great Britain
by Amazon